March 6

DR. MELLON OF HAITI

Also by Peter Michelmore

Einstein, Profile of the Man

DR. MELLON OF HAITI

PETER MICHELMORE

Illustrated with photographs

DODD, MEAD & COMPANY, NEW YORK

Library of Congress Catalog Card Number: 64-22401

Printed in the United States of America
by The Cornwall Press, Inc., Cornwall, N. Y.

AUTHOR'S NOTE

William Larimer Mellon, Jr., was on a flying visit to New York when I first approached him about writing a book on his hospital in Haiti. He was not at all enthusiastic.

"I don't need the publicity," he told me over the telephone. "And the hospital doesn't need the publicity."

However, over a period of time and after several interviews, he lost his objections to the book. Some of his staff were wary, never quite convinced that Mellon had agreed to the project, but the man himself could not have been more helpful.

I cannot be certain why Mellon allowed me to proceed. He is a great student of Albert Schweitzer and he knows that fame has been a burden to the doctor of Lambaréné. For this reason Mellon has desired to remain as anonymous as possible and has several times refused to permit television documentaries and magazine articles on his hospital. Why a book? Now I think it over, I believe Mellon may have co-operated with me because I became a friend and the thing of most value he could give me, as a writer, was his own story. To put it mildly, Mellon is a generous man.

I thank Dr. Mellon for his gift.

My appreciation also to Gwen Mellon and her daughter

Jenny; to Matthew Mellon and his sister, Peggy Hitchcock; to Emory Ross and Charlie Ponte and Andy Gallagher and Chuck Wiggin and Pastor Bois and Julian Strauss and Miss Walborg Peterson; and to my friends, the Diederichs Bernard and Ginette.

A hundred people contributed in one way or another to this book. Eliani guided me far into the Haitian hills. Caroline took me across banana fields and through rivers to her mission in Haiti's far north. Maurice Angus rescued me one night when I was stranded in Saint Marc, and a planter named Staley Pitts performed the same service at Pont Sonde. My thanks also to Bob Miot and Paul Cummings who shared their accommodations with me during visits to Deschapelles.

Among the permanent doctors at Deschapelles, Harold May and Gérard Frédérique devoted many hours to assisting me with my research. Only a handful of doctors are named in this book, but they can be taken to represent the scores who have served at Deschapelles for various periods. Dr. Robert Hollister and his wife Cornelia were particularly kind to me and greatly helped my project.

Haiti is a dictatorship where terror and graft are freely practiced by the people in power. It has always been this way in Haiti and perhaps it always will be. It does not improve the condition of four million Haitian peasants for outsiders to make literary capital out of the sad political climate, nor does it help Mellon's cause. I have written of politics in this book only where it is absolutely essential to the narrative, and I wish to state that none of this political material was discussed with anyone at any time at Deschapelles. It was obvious, without asking, that the attitude of the Americans at Deschapelles is that Haiti is for the Haitians to govern—or misgovern. This is an attitude with which I fully agree.

To anticipate readers' requests about how to contribute to

AUTHOR'S NOTE

Larry Mellon's work in Haiti, I might add that checks may be sent to The Grant Foundation, P.O. Box 1138, Pittsburgh, Pennsylvania.

PETER MICHELMORE

Adelaide,
Australia

ILLUSTRATIONS

DR. MELLON OF HAITI

IT WAS LATE in the afternoon, but still very hot and dusty so that his hands were moist and gritty on the steering wheel. His faded blue shirt was clammy with sweat and he sat forward in the seat, allowing the breeze through the open window of the moving car to cool his back. His face, flushed with the heat, was set with fatigue and there was a slight slump to the shoulders. He looked his fifty-three years, although his face was lean, with regular features, and his eyes were clear behind the dark-rimmed glasses. He was hatless and his thin white hair ruffled in the wind.

The road was not paved and the unchromed white Chevrolet kicked up a swirl of white dust that settled on the blue-green scrub bushes on either side. The dust was inside the car, too, coating the man's shoes. They were excellent shoes, handmade dark tan brogues, the sort sold by Abercrombie & Fitch.

When the car slowed down to pass through a village a few of the peasants waved and called, *"Bo'soir, Docteur."* Some of the children, who did not know that this was Dr. Mellon, shouted, "Hey, *blanc,*" the way they hailed all white men. Mellon raised his hand to return the greetings, but he did not stop. He was anxious to get home to Deschapelles.

In the quiet early morning, with dew on the grass and the tropic night smell of fresh vanilla lingering, a Haitian village could seem picturesque. At this hour, however, the harsh light showed up the dilapidated daub-and-thatch huts and scrappy cactus hedgerows in full squalor.

Peasants lived in the dirt here as they did in a thousand other villages in Haiti. They were hungry, poor, diseased. Four million Negro peasants in a crumpled, worn-out, unvisited land in the Caribbean, and few outsiders cared whether they lived or died. Conveniently out of sight of the rest of the world, they were nobody's responsibility, except—perhaps—that of the capital city, Port-au-Prince. And Port-au-Prince cared least of all. The peasants were stupid big-toed Negroes and their poverty was self-inflicted, went the argument. They had kept on breeding children and splitting up the land into smaller and smaller pieces until there were families of eight or nine scratching about on an acre of soil that had been sucked dry a generation ago. Nor did they seem to strive to improve their lot. Wait and see, they said, and left their future to the favors of the voodoo spirits and the *grand* God. "*Bon Dieu bon, bon Dieu bon:* (God is good . . . God is good)." A hundred times a day they said it to reassure themselves that there was some mercy in the world. Yet the mercy rarely arrived. When a hurricane flattened peasant villages in the south and left thousands maimed and starving, neighboring countries rushed in relief food supplies. Trucks rolled out of Port-au-Prince for the south, but they were hijacked within miles and the food was put on the black market. The crime brought shrugs in Haiti. No one on earth was more expendable than a Haitian peasant.

Mellon had some of these thoughts as he drove through

the village, braking frequently to avoid the chickens and piglets scuttling under his wheels. Here and there, tending open cooking fires, peasant women squatted wearily with the folds of their dresses tucked between their thighs. Naked children chased about, legs and arms smeared with the gray dust from the beaten ground around the huts. The men stood about, talking. When night came, in the shuttered sweating darkness of those huts the men would be making love to the women, recklessly, having no thought of the children they could never feed properly. One man might have three women pregnant at once.

By God, how Mellon wished sometimes that the peasants had more reason, more ambition, showed some sign of marching into the twentieth century. But he knew this could not be, and he accepted it. What he would not accept was the decay and death. He could not see the Haitians collectively as a horde of downtrodden, faceless black people. To him they were all individuals with names and families and separate pains, fears and hopes. They were people with the will to live and to enjoy life. His task was to buttress that will and to help sustain and nourish life.

That was why he had come to Haiti, why he was still there. No matter how many obstacles were put in Mellon's path whether by his own shortcomings or by the people he sought to help, no matter how large loomed the magnitude of the task, there was no question of his giving up. For it was because too few cared about the peasants that they had drifted into their present shambles.

They had been kept ignorant and leaderless. Nobody had told them that they were imprisoned in an ailing land deceived into believing that they could garden and dance and make love to their heart's content. They had never been warned that Haiti was a tight little country, nor that their villages were multiplied over and over through the land and that the multiplication would go on until they all suffocated.

The Negroes had come to Haiti as slaves and won their freedom in a bloody struggle, thus creating the world's first black republic. But one wondered about this freedom. The eternal dictatorship in Port-au-Prince had affixed the chains of poverty and ignorance as firmly as the chains of iron of old. A century and a half after independence most Haitians were still in bondage.

By detaching himself from politics and working on the personal level, Mellon had found a method that enabled him to help right the wrong done these people. He was only one man of peace and he could not heal all Haiti, but he had made a start.

What Mellon had done was to map out a small section of the island for urgent succor, an area in the middle of the country comprising about two hundred square miles and containing 75,000 people. Roughly, it took in the district of Verrettes, including part of the Artibonite Valley and some of the mountains to the south: just a corner of this land, Mellon told himself, but soon we may "adopt" more. This dream was dashed, for Mellon had had to push all his resources to the limit to tend his one tiny province.

In 1956, he had built a hospital at Deschapelles in the center of the district, yet this did not seem nearly enough. Over the years he established schools and village literacy sessions, laid pipelines to carry clean water to the market places, created jobs for peasants in sewing and cotton weaving, taught them how to raise pigs, even built latrines.

He had begun as a rich man. Now he was poor and selling off hospital vehicles and cutting supplies. His heart had faltered once with exhaustion, but he blamed it on coffee. Doctors and field officers came and went, but Mellon and his wife had kept on, pouring themselves into what had become an urgent and immense rescue operation.

All this, and people still told Mellon he was wasting his time. One of his doctors had just quit. "Dr. Mellon," he said, "what you're doing here is trying to empty an ocean of misery with a teacup. You're not getting anywhere. I think I can be more useful back in the States."

Mellon simply told the man that he himself felt differently. He shook the doctor's hand and said good-bye, no hard feelings. What Mellon needed was help; other men must give themselves unconditionally to the Haitians without concern for personal justification. Yet he never said this to anyone. It was up to a man to work out his duties for himself. Mellon disliked evangelism.

Yet discouragement was a constant obstacle. Take, for instance, this day coming so soon after his associate's dampening resignation. Out in the valley, checking on a half dozen of his projects, Mellon found that a water pipeline he had laid to a school had sprung a leak. The Haitians were standing around waiting for him to happen by to fix it. Then one of the girls who had worked at the hospital stopped him on the road and told him she was going to Nassau by sailboat from the northern town of Port-de-Paix. This was the underground out of Haiti for desperate peasants who imagined the Bahamas to be more of a Promised Land. The escape route was expensive and dangerous.

What concerned Mellon most were the girl's three illegitimate children. She was leaving them with a sister who was already overburdened with a family of her own and an invalid mother. Mellon knew he could not change the girl's decision. "You'll drown," he said drily. Then he added, "But I'll pray for you."

Much of the afternoon he had spent digging a deep GI latrine near a peasant family compound of several huts. Peasants usually defecated in the woods or the cane fields, but this was an open section and the mess was near the living quarters where the children played. One youngster had already been to the hospital with typhoid. For weeks after he had instructed the men on how to build a latrine and fence it around with a wooden shack, nothing had been done. Today he had grabbed a pick and shovel out of his car trunk and started digging himself. The Haitians finally rallied to take a turn, but Mellon set the pace and stayed around until the rough timbers were being put into place and the latrine nearly completed.

It had been a rugged afternoon and Mellon, who had rarely driven five uninterrupted miles in the valley since he arrived, was determined to go straight home and forget the trials of the day with a shower and an hour before dinner, playing his flute on the cool, hidden patio.

At the edge of the village, however, outside a primitive mill piled with sacks of rice and corn, a gray-haired Haitian flagged down the car. He walked to the driver's side and touched his forehead in salute.

"Bo'soir, Docteur," he said. Speaking in soft Creole, the Negro identified himself as the owner of the mill, then started an account of a former employee who had become a helpless cripple and needed somebody to look after him. The man

was friendless and destitute. "Can I bring him to your hospital?" he asked.

Mellon had listened attentively, nodding to show that he understood and was very sorry to hear about the cripple. He really had no defense against tales of suffering like this. The pity had come up into his eyes. But at the sudden question, an impatient frown crossed his face as he said, "Why don't you look after him yourself?"

The Negro did not acknowledge the rebuff. He thanked Mellon for his time and stepped back, gesturing the car on with his hand.

Damn it, thought Mellon as he accelerated, when will these people accept some responsibility for their own? It lasted about a mile, this attempt to reason his rudeness. Then he began berating himself for letting his drear mood overcome his civility, and he worried about the fate of the old cripple. The incident stayed in his mind as he turned off the limestone road at the big corner tree with the weathered signboard: Hôpital Albert Schweitzer. Glumly he drove the half mile up the rutted track toward Deschapelles, then swung left beneath the stone arch that dated back to French colonial days, and headed up and around the driveway on to the cobbled courtyard by his shaded bungalow. In the open garage he turned off the engine and sat staring straight ahead for a full minute, while two tawny dogs yapped at the car door.

The next morning he drove back to the village to find the Haitian with the gray hair. He was not at the mill and it took a long search to find his house.

Courteously, as before, the man brushed aside Mellon's apology. "All I want to know," he said, "is whether something can be done for the fellow to make him more self-sufficient." For four years this Haitian had been feeding the man out of a special disaster fund created for his employees by putting aside ten per cent of his mill profits each year. The mill was small and he made a bare living, so the fund was not large. This one man had been a severe drain on the money, penalizing other workmen in need.

On the beach at Saint Marc, Mellon found the cripple sitting forlornly in the sand. He had no clothes. Both legs were shrunken from some previous illness and one leg was twisted under his body, immovable now from sheer inactivity. Mellon took him in the car back to the hospital, dressed him in clean pajamas, and put him to bed. A visiting orthopedic surgeon was called in; and after careful examination he decided that he could straighten the man's leg with surgery, allowing him to walk on crutches and return to light work at the mill.

It was the mill owner, not Mellon, who had been the hero of this little drama. The shoestring welfare program had touched Mellon deeply and the spring returned to his step when he left the hospital and followed the back trail across the creek to his house. Now it was Mellon and the mill owner who cared about saving these people. And what about Monsieur Delinois and his Old Folks' Home? Pastor Bois and his new orphanage? And Jerome, Pierre, and the others who were building the TB village? All these men and doubtless many more he did not know, who would go through life with only a few peasants seeing their nobility. If he was trying to empty the ocean with a teacup, there were other fools attempting the same impossible task.

At home, Mellon leafed through one of Albert Schweitzer's

books until he came to the passage he wanted. He transcribed it into the thin green notebook he carried in his pocket.

"There are no heroes of action," wrote Schweitzer, "only heroes of renunciation and suffering. Of such there are plenty. But few of them are known and even these not to the crowd but to the few."

2

Although Mellon had been accused of being "soft" on the Haitians, refusing to admit their torpor, he was as aware as anyone else of the suffering and shabbiness of his adopted land. The difference was that he did not allow it to overwhelm him. He looked beyond the gloom and found a purity that honestly lifted his soul.

It was there, in the crowd, one clinic day at the hospital, a clinic day that dawned like hundreds of others, with the morning sun coming up over the bare hills, burning the mist out of the valley and blazing down on wretchedness everywhere.

Four hundred peasants were converging on Deschapelles, straggling down from the hills and trekking across the floor of the valley. They fixed their eyes on the distant silver water tower that glinted above the dark green tropic trees and made for it the best way they could, pushing through fields of tall millet, jamming into the ancient ferry punt across the Artibonite River, filing along the narrow trails through the rice paddies. Some were packed into trucks and making the journey along the pebbled roads from Verrettes or Saint Marc. Most walked, however, or rode on the backs of horses and mules. One man, tied down and delirious with gangrene, had been carried all the way from the mountains on a litter. Another, with a failing heart, was being gentled along in a makeshift sedan chair.

People with malaria, tuberculosis, diabetes, cancer, typhoid, broken limbs, bodies rotten with worms, bellies corroded with hunger, and some grotesque afflictions straight out of the Old Testament—all moved on Deschapelles. One woman was hurrying there to desert her diseased baby on the hospital steps, and a girl with syphilis was cursing her pregnancy with every step. They shared the path with a weeping mother who cradled her infant daughter, quivering with tetanus. Following the bloody footsteps of a shuffling boy with open ulcers on his legs was a young man hunched with burning gonorrhea, and then a ten-year-old boy leading his blind mother by the hand.

The water tower was their landmark. Beneath, splendidly cool and clean among lawns and scrubbed cobbled courtyards, was the hospital that Mellon built.

By nine o'clock, the scatter of travelers had become a throng and the peasants were upon the hospital. They crowded into the wire-screened waiting room with its Roman benches and they sprawled on the broad steps outside. A young nurse, who had just arrived from Schweitzer's hospital in Africa, walked up from the wards to view this scene for the first time. She lifted a hand to her face. "Dear God!" she cried.

She saw misery that ate away at the heart and bowels, all the more terrible because much of it could have been prevented if the peasants had not been kept in their prison of ignorance. They did not even know enough not to drink from the same stream in which they had urinated.

Here was one of the worst scenes in Haiti—not *the* worst by any means—yet Mellon, who had witnessed it countless times, did not despair. He was running a field hospital on a battleground: the peasants against poverty and hunger. If the need for the hospital had been less urgent, he might not be there. Wave after wave of peasants came to Deschapelles to be patched up to continue the battle: 70,000 different people since the hospital opened and most of these several times. Always the scene was grim on clinic mornings, but by the end of the day, there would be some laughter and much fresh hope.

Crushing adversity had made some of those who came hard, mean, and cruel. But in many others the natural simplicity, grace, and gaiety of the Haitian peasant had survived. Perhaps these people were hopelessly naive; perhaps also this was the reason they could bear so much. In any case, Mellon worked to sustain this spirit. To him, it was enchanting.

And on this particular day enchantment wore a straw hat and her name was Clotilde.

She was young and slender and she walked along the road with a nonchalant and sensual stride that some women can never effect in years of trying. Her head was high, her back straight and steady. All the movement came from the hips, from the supple, pert, feminine swing that made her dress sway.

For three miles she had walked. But even so far from home, she was recognized by a few as she passed by the chattering market place under the fig tree.

"*Bonjou'*, Clotilde," a woman of about fifty with a kerchief tied around her head called from her wicker chair. She sat beneath a ragged palm-leaf shelter and the counter in front of her was neatly arranged with white bread loaves, candy sticks, soaps, buttons, and pocketbook mirrors.

"*Bonjou'*, Madame Orius." Clotilde loved to be greeted.

The woman watched after the girl with a wrinkle of approval under her eyes. God, she may well have thought, made nothing more exquisite than a pretty *Négresse*.

The smooth, dark brown face of the girl had luster at the cheeks and in the center of the forehead. Her eyes shone, too, and were brown and warm, with curling eyelashes. The nose and chin were fine-boned. A straw hat perched on her head. Her cheap silver earrings danced. She wore her best dress, a faded blue cotton with clean white piping at the hems. It was patched here and there and each of the buttonholes down the front was frayed and torn.

Clotilde's eyes lingered on the new dresses of bottle green and bright red that were spread out on a straw mat at the edge of the market. Not today. All the money she had in the world was the fistful of coins she had borrowed from her sister, and she needed this. Clotilde had waited at her home market while her sister haggled and clucked and besought people to buy from her basket of sweet green oranges. Slowly, a few cents at a time, the money had accumulated until the sister had earned two gourdes for Clotilde.

The silver coins were hot and moist in Clotilde's hand. It had been a long walk. She lowered her eyes now against the low sun to glimpse the long stone pavilions through the trees. Across the bridge she walked, past the fountain that gushed pure spring water all day long, then into the shade of the big flamboyat trees. A dirt track cut to the left along a twisted post and rail fence. Clotilde took this track and quickened her step at the sight of the people milling ahead. She was on the driveway now, skipping past a ramshackle bus that positively bulged with people. To her right was an open shelter with block lettering carved in the main concrete beam.

Although Clotilde could not read she knew that this was Madame Mellon's Hospital. What the lettering actually said was HÔPITAL ALBERT SCHWEITZER, but most of the peasants called it "Madame Mellon's Hospital" after the gauntly beautiful white woman who was always somewhere there in the corridors, or perched on a stool behind the reception counter, or translating the peasant Creole into English for the *blanc* doctor in the baby clinic. The hospital was also called simply "Deschapelles," which had been the name of this part of the valley for as long as anybody could remember. In fact, the name went back a full two hundred years, to some forgotten Frenchman called Deschapelles who ran a plantation here with slave labor.

Many times before, Clotilde had been to Deschapelles and she was trained so well in what to do that there was a trace of haughtiness about her when she walked inside the waiting room and up to the long counter to register with Jerome Jean-Baptiste. He was, as usual, all business, this brown man with the strong face and frank eyes. With only the faintest nod of recognition, he checked her white rendezvous card and sent her along the desk to pay her visiting fee of two gourdes and have her name written in a book. All this routine was pleasing to Clotilde. She had real identity here. A brisk young Haitian found Clotilde's medical folder in the filing cabinet, stamped a new sheet SURGERY, and sent the document off to the doctor. The slender girl who had caused this activity went now to the end of the hall and found a place for herself on a wooden seat against the wall.

The blunt clinical language in Clotilde's case history folder gave the barest biography, but some of it may have matched her thoughts as she sat waiting, her dress smoothed down over her comely legs and her hat still high on her head. . . .

So-called elite mulattoes and Negroes in Port-au-Prince, Gonaïves, and other Haitian towns would have described Clotilde as a no-account peasant girl just by two words in her dossier. Against marital status was typed "concubine," and against employment, *cultivatrice.*

This was enough for them to call up images of primitive wattle huts, mangy dogs, tired fields of Congo beans and millet, Saturday nights at the voodoo dances, dusty markets, sweating dusks, and the disheveled sleeping-mat freshening in the morning sun. It was life too close to the bone.

To be sure, there had been some sweetness to it in time gone by. Peasant families once gathered at twilight, bellies full and a pipe for the old man, and told hilarious stories about Bouki and Ti Malice, two Haitian folk characters who were constantly getting into scrapes that brought out Bouki's fantastic stupidity and Ti Malice's outrageous cunning. But it was difficult to act out a funny story on an empty stomach. Today hunger spoiled everything. Peasant children growing up were more likely to have bitter memories of family arguments over food than gay recollections of the Bouki tales.

Clotilde had had little time for light-heartedness. At every opportunity she toiled in the fields, fed her children as best she could and submitted her body to a man at night—not just any man but the one with whom she was going steady. Until he left her, she would be faithful. She would have preferred a permanent man and a wedding ring, but how many could afford the ceremony and the ring, and how many girls could find a man who would be satisfied with one woman?

So Clotilde was a concubine with work-worn hands who had first become pregnant at fourteen and had loved and been loved by men ever since. Now twenty-four, she had had five children by three different men. But she also had her own *caille* (hut) now, and her own little garden. She was a *Négresse* of some prestige. It was with immense pride that she took in her fourth man and his three children and gave them a home, although this was not very practical. The tiny garden could not feed a family of ten, and there was scant work available in the valley that would let Clotilde and her man earn the money to buy food. The family had to ration itself to only one decent meal a day, yet Clotilde had survived much tougher times and she was not complaining.

Through the shadows of life, as she saw it now, there was the bright light of the hospital. She had told her sister once that she was in love with Deschapelles, and then giggled because it sounded so girlish. But she meant it just the same. . . .

Like everyone else in her community, Clotilde was nominally a Catholic. What she really believed, however, was that good and evil, happiness and sorrow, depended on the assortment of voodoo gods who handled worldly affairs for the Number One God. In times of trouble and sickness, the peasants appealed for help to the appropriate voodoo spirit, using as an intermediary a *houngan* or witch doctor. The price of this comfort often came high, for many *houngans* were rascals and charged exorbitant fees. So now Clotilde and other poverty-stricken peasants were increasingly less able to afford the luxury of a voodoo priest. For them, the establishment of the hospital in the valley came as a special blessing. Even if the white doctors worked on an entirely physical level and could not possibly reach some sicknesses, they had certain cures for other ailments. The hospital brought a degree of security and refuge that the peasant's life had lacked before.

Clotilde had first sought this refuge out of desperation some seven years earlier. A local *bocor,* a herb doctor, had given her a potion for an aching tooth. The bitter juice eased the ache, but her body erupted in an ugly burning rash which the *bocor* could not pretend to cure. A neighbor who had visited the new hospital—and who talked about the experience at every opportunity—urged Clotilde to visit Deschapelles. She would need her paper, her tattered birth certificate, to convince that emphatic man Jean-Baptiste she really lived in the district. He had sent away people from distant places, even rich people. And Clotilde would need three gourdes—about sixty cents—for the first visit.

Well, she had gone through the ordeal, waited hours in a room more crowded than a market, and finally had seen a white doctor, only to be told that her rash would vanish if she simply stopped taking her toothache potion. Then the rash went and the toothache returned. This time, however, Clotilde had bypassed the *bocor* and gone straight to Deschapelles where a dentist removed the bad tooth.

Stomach pains, dizziness, and an all-over feeling of absolute misery sent her to the hospital again a year later. She saw Madame Mellon's man, Dr. Mellon, and he had kneaded her belly, checked her blood pressure, listened to her through his stethoscope—in short had given her the full treatment she had heard so much about. More than that, Dr. Mellon authorized her to visit the hospital for an injection of penicillin on each of the next ten days. A *pici-pici* (injection) was the ultimate magic. Peasants had become familiar with the hypodermic needle some years before when Dr. François Duvalier himself led a yaws campaign right through the country. There had been a spectacular victory over this vile disease of the skin, and now Dr. Duvalier was President of Haiti.

The *pici-pici* worked for Clotilde, too, and she was to have many injections over the years as the pain chased around her body, from her pelvic bone to her breast and to her teeth again. She was afflicted with jaundice, malaria, and terrible sickness during her pregnancies. At one time, soon after her second man had left her, she was almost ready to die. But then Dr. Mellon had helped with money and, unknown to her, had scrawled a brief unmedical postscript in her dossier: "No appetite—no husband—three little kids to look after . . ."

So it was largely because of the hospital at Deschapelles that Clotilde was able to weather the hard years. Sometimes she had the chance to attend voodoo ceremonies and dance herself into abandon and escape from her problems. Still, she was looking to the hospital more and more for wellbeing of spirit as well as of body.

Some peasants with a disease waited too long before going to Deschapelles. Very often the doctors said they could not be cured. Clotilde, on the other hand, bustled off to the clinic like a suburban housewife whenever she or the children became slightly ill. And all five of her children had stayed alive. This in itself was an achievement—this keeping peasant children alive in Haiti. Some girls in Clotilde's little neighborhood of Moro-Desil had lost three out of five children to disease.

Clotilde had fended for herself for a long time, one young peasant woman against a wall of hardship. She had not been able to accumulate many possessions and her most extravagant dream was still to own a horse, but she was winning her battle with life. . . .

Now it was near Christmas. Her garden was bare, and there was no money and no food in the house. Her new man was kind and ready to work, but he was a stranger to the district and could not find any sort of job. Clotilde knew a family along the road with three acres of rice coming into grain, and she coaxed them into hiring the two of them to help with the harvest. The small wages for both would carry them over the lean spell.

A week before harvest time, Clotilde had stumbled in a field. A stiff millet leaf pierced her ankle. The cut was deep and the blood flowed. At Deschapelles she had the wound dressed and was given a shot of penicillin and a tetanus antitoxin injection. Keep the ankle out of dirt and water, she was advised. Obviously she could not work in a rice paddy.

The prospect of losing such a hard-found prize as a harvest job depressed Clotilde for days, but then she noticed that her wound was healing over very well and that it was not tender to walk on. Time, however, was against her. Her man had started to harvest the rice down the road. Unless Clotilde could begin work immediately a replacement would have to be found for her.

So the doctor's decision on this particular clinic morning, eight days after the accident, was vitally important to Clotilde.

She left her seat after a while and hovered at the doctor's door, waiting for her name to be called. Inside the small spartan room, Dr. Harold May, an American, and Nurse Louise Rémy, a Haitian, were examining the patients with a swift thoroughness they had acquired in a long Deschapelles clinical partnership. They were never brusque, these two. Miss Rémy had a classic Creole face—the proud lift, olive skin, high cheekbones, and black hair combed tightly back. It was magnificent, *formidable*. Clotilde had been in awe of Miss Rémy at first, but then she had discovered how easily she smiled. About Dr. May there was no mystery. He was the chief surgeon at Deschapelles and, excepting only Dr. Mellon, he was the gentlest American the peasants had ever encountered. If anyone had told them about some of the operations he had to perform, they would not have believed it of him.

Suddenly Clotilde's turn came. Remembering the ankle injury, Dr. May bent and ran his fingers over the wound. "Okay, cherie," he said, and then, in Creole, he prescribed for her another shot of penicillin and regular hot soaks for the ankle. Clotilde sat forward, her hands clasped before her, and her hat now a little askew on her head. Tears brimmed in her eyes. She must be allowed to work in the paddy field, she said. There was no money in the house. She owed her sister two gourdes. The doctor just had to say yes.

Listening to this peasant girl pleading for the privilege of breaking her back from dawn to dusk in a sticky rice paddy, Harold May had an almost overpowering desire to reach into his pocket and give her the few dollars she stood to make. But the steel in Clotilde forbade an act of charity. May felt he had no right to offer her anything but her chance to work, and this, thankfully, he could give her because the risk of infection had passed. When she left the room, May watched the empty doorway for a full minute before he called the next patient.

Within an hour, Clotilde was home. She checked to see that the older children were keeping the infants out of trouble. Then she took off her best blue dress and sandals and shimmied into an old calico smock. Down the road she went at a run, turning off into a rice field toward the tall, bare-chested figure of her man. When he saw her coming, he called something in Creole. Clotilde broke step and pretended to limp. Then she shouted with laughter and jumped up and down to show that her ankle was sound. They came together and joined hands, whooping with glee and dancing a ring-around-a-rosy in the black mud.

3

A HAITIAN NIGHT is still, starlit, strange; it calls a lull in a struggle for existence waged openly only under the sun. Night brings a truce and then gets on with a life of its own, a life that is heard but not seen. The warm air shudders with the piercing shrill of a million cicadas and the echoing rattle of voodoo drums across the valley. Like pistol shots from a cane thicket somewhere off in the distance, the whip cracks again and again as a peasant boy drives a yoked mule around and around the turning mahogany hub of an old sugar mill.

At the Deschapelles hospital, two doctors lay on their backs on the roof, their hands behind their heads. They were gazing up at the night and listening. For an hour they had not spoken a word to each other.

Far down the road a white Chevrolet ghosted along and the man at the wheel, after a long silence, began to talk softly to his companion about other times and other places, tracing the events that had made him a part of this unearthly night.

"I was born in opulence," said William Larimer Mellon,

Jr., choosing the word deliberately and making it sound distasteful.

He was the fourth child of William Larimer and Mary Mellon. This placed him deep in the bosom of America's Mellon clan during its most acquisitive era—the time when only a corporation or two separated it from the richness of the Rockefellers.

The family fortune was started by Thomas Mellon, who in 1818 migrated from Protestant Ireland to Pennsylvania, where he used what he called his "spirit and energy" to change his occupation from farmer to real-estate tycoon, banker, and lawyer. The third of his five sons was Andrew W. Mellon, the financial genius who in time took over the Mellon bank and then applied his Midas touch to oil, coal, steel, trains, aluminum, bridges—everything. He also kept an eye on his older brother James, a compulsive philanthropist who frequently had to be restrained. But James's son, William Larimer, was the favorite of old Thomas.

Young "W.L.," as he was known, received twenty thousand dollars from his grandfather for a twenty-first birthday gift. He used it to sink an oil well and scored a gusher. On such luck and Mellon shrewdness was the Gulf Oil Company founded, with W.L. as president.

Despite his strictly businesslike and Presbyterian approach to life, W.L. was influenced by one trait of his father's. James had married purely for love, rather than in the tradition, established by old Thomas, of acquiring a strong woman to beget sons. So Mary Taylor, a gentle Scots-American girl, became the mistress of "Ben Elm," W.L.'s great stone mansion overlooking the drab and unkempt city of Pittsburgh.

None of the family liked ostentation, least of all Mary Taylor Mellon. She would not wear any jewelry, shunned the social circuit and devoted most of her time to her family, her church, and her music. Her father, who built asphalt sidewalks in Brooklyn, had insisted that every member of his family play a musical instrument. Mary's main talent, however, was her soprano voice. She liked to sing herself and to hear others singing.

That night, in Haiti, Larimer Mellon lapsed back into silence when he remembered his mother. She had been staunch, tender, and he felt—or hoped—that he had been greatly influenced by her character. With fondness in his voice, he spoke then of a cruise in the Caribbean on his father's yacht and of his mother taking him by the hand one night and tiptoeing him forward to listen to the low soft spirituals sung by the Bahamian crew.

The cruises on the *Vagabondia* and the holidays on a private island in Canada were the memorable times in what must have been a lonely boyhood for young Larry. W. L. was busy with his oil and then with local Republican politics after his uncle Andrew W. went to Washington as Secretary of the Treasury. After a series of sicknesses, Mary became an invalid and was often away in hospitals. Peggy Mellon was nine years older than Larry and the other two children, Rachel and Matthew, were older still. Larry had his early schooling from a French governess and later prepped at Choate.

"There were times," said Larimer Mellon, "when I felt ashamed to be from a family that was known only for wealth.

I felt more at home with chambermaids than with people in my own group."

He rebelled when his father insisted he go to college, but finally agreed to try Princeton for a year. If he did not like it, he would be allowed to join one of the Mellon business enterprises.

This was 1928 and Mellon found it all ineffably dull. "I wanted no part of it, not even the sports," he said. "I was nearly drummed out because I didn't take part in sports, but I settled the argument by doing a little gymnastics. I took the general arts course like most of them, at least most of the Pittsburgh crowd. In those days everyone wanted to be a bond salesman and belong to the right clubs. That was the limit of their ambition. I didn't know what I wanted, but I knew I wouldn't get it at Princeton. I quit after that first year and went to work in the Mellon bank."

Young Mellon found a second home at this time in a small shingled place, owned by the Rowley family, in the Pittsburgh suburbs. The father earned a frugal living by making artificial limbs; the mother kept a warm kitchen, with homely conversation and hot coffee always on tap. There was a calico- and fresh-baked-bread atmosphere about the house that the rich youth from "Ben Elm" found delicious. It only deepened his infatuation with the Rowleys' pretty blonde, seventeen-year-old daughter, Grace, who had taken him there in the first place.

Old Thomas Mellon had written in his family log: "Level-headed young people avoid escapades and elopements or thoughts of suicide—such courses are for weaklings."

His great-grandson, aged nineteen, took no notice. In the

early winter of 1929, when the rest of the clan was busy buttressing its empire after the stock market crash, Larimer skipped down to Wellsburg, West Virginia, and married Grace Rowley on the sly. He hid away his bride in a little bungalow outside Pittsburgh while he wondered how he would tell his parents. The only Mellon to be let in on the secret was his brother Matthew, eleven years his senior, another Mellon misfit who was then teaching American philosophy in Germany. W.L. had had trouble with both sons. When Matthew had chosen an academic career instead of Gulf Oil, the father had turned to Larimer, who was also proving to be a disappointment. For all his austerity of manner, W.L. loved his family. Whatever their interests he wanted his boys to be good friends; he had continually sought to strengthen the relationship between the two brothers. But although Matthew had a blustering sort of regard for his brother and was amused by the news of the secret marriage, he was outwardly disapproving.

"With that moral streak of his, Larry wouldn't live with the girl unless he married her," Matthew says now. "It proved to be a big mistake." Actually Matthew has a rather libelous view of the whole episode. But the essential detail was that Larry bided his time for nearly a year, then announced to his parents that he wanted to marry Grace. The Mellons arranged a formal wedding and sent out invitations. It would be the social event of the season. A few days before the wedding, a Presbyterian minister down in Wellsburg called in reporters and said he had married the young couple the previous winter. The wedding was called off and the invited guests angrily took back their presents.

Remarkably forgiving, W. L. Mellon offered to give the

couple a new home as a marriage gift. He asked his teenage daughter-in-law what sort of house she would like. "I prefer French château architecture," she replied, which was the most un-Mellonlike statement ever heard at "Ben Elm."

In Matthew's opinion, Grace was "not up to" the challenge of marrying into so much affluence. Luxury went to her head. Larry's dream of a cozy homespun life came to naught, for his wife sought the opposite.

"How I hated all those parties," he said. "Year after year the same people danced with the same people and they had the same conversations. I came to despise that jaded group of remittance people who lived on trust accounts and did little else. It was my feeling that a man should try to do something on his own. He could be a professional baseball player or a carpenter. It didn't matter what, just so long as a man was using his own talents. Nobody has much respect for a kept woman and neither should they have for a kept man. He doesn't deserve respect."

Larry moved from the bank to the statistical department of Gulf Oil, but the change did not help his discontent. He and Grace had a son, Billy, but even the baby did not ease his restlessness. He yearned to be in the outdoors and was happiest at the weekends when he wandered the Pennsylvania countryside on horseback. Driving back to Pittsburgh after one of these jaunts with his mare Goldy in the horse trailer behind his car, he made his decision to move west and take up ranching.

W.L. thought it was a rotten idea. Ranching was dirty work, and as a business proposition it was risky. But W.L. knew that the Mellons were a stubborn breed and he let Larimer have his head.

So, knowing, too, that what he wanted most was to escape from his marriage, Larry hitched the horse trailer on his station wagon, pitched in some straw for Goldy, and took off alone.

"If you're going to buy a ranch, you might just as well buy one with oil potential," one of the Gulf Oil field managers in Texas told the Easterner when he arrived in the summer of 1935. "Now I don't know if there is any grass on it, but Pecos County has great oil potential. Buy there and, if you fail in cattle, you are sure to get your money back in oil."

Pecos County proved to be grassless and Larry went on into Arizona and bought himself a spread near Rimrock. Within a few years the big oil boom hit Pecos County. Had Larry followed the Gulf man's advice, he reckoned later, he could have bought the whole state of Arizona.

"But this might have spoiled a pretty fair ranch hand," he says.

Right from the start he stuck doggedly to the frontier idea that the only way to run a ranch was from the saddle. In deference to the modern trend he sometimes substituted a dump truck for his horse, but the principle was the same. There was a thin margin of profit in raising cattle then and it would not support what Larry called a flashy operation.

He did his own fencing, his own branding. When it was time to drive the cattle down from the hills to winter pasture, it was Larry who rode herd the longest hours each day. He slept in the open, was the first man at the chuck wagon every morning. At the main ranch his only indulgence was a rough-hewn shack. According to his sister Peggy, it was a "one-peg shack" and the peg was usually empty because there was nothing to hang on it. He kept his spare Levi's and shirts in a duffel bag, ever ready to be pulled shut and thrown into the back of the truck.

Cowhands who worked at the ranch long remembered the opening remark of the young man's mother on her first visit: "Oh, son, really!" The reaction of Larry's wife was more emphatic. She took one look, then scurried back to Pittsburgh and sued for divorce.

There was very little beef of his own on the ranch in the early years, but Larry made reasonable profits fattening cattle for ranchers in Old Mexico. All his money was used to enlarge his property holdings. In 1938, he persuaded his father to buy enough cattle to stock his land for fifty per cent of the proceeds. W.L.'s luck was never sour. Beef prices went higher and higher. He made a killing when, at best, he expected to break even.

Increased profits, however, did nothing to influence Larry's mode of living. When his sister Peggy came visiting, he moved out of the single-bed shack and slept with the horses.

Peggy noted that he got up at five o'clock every morning and went to bed with the chickens, too tired to think of reading a book. She thought her brother was wasting himself but she did not say anything.

On one occasion the family persuaded the cowboy to join them for a fishing trip off the coast of Lower California. Larry's entire wardrobe was, as usual, in the duffel bag he hoisted aboard. W.L. guessed at his son's measurements and radioed ahead to Los Angeles for a tailor to meet the yacht with two suits. Duly presented with the new clothes, Larry was abashed. "Gee, I have nowhere to keep suits," he said. "I haven't got any hangers."

Larry was enjoying the life of a cowboy too much to think of marrying again—at least until he met the classically pretty woman who had taken a job as riding instructress on a dude ranch near his own. Her name was Gwen Grant Rawson and she had come to Arizona to set up residence for a divorce. She was also supporting three youngsters—Michael, Jennifer, and Ian—and had to take any work she could get.

"I understand you have three children," Larry said by way of an opening conversation. "I'd like to meet them." Despite his leathery, rangy appearance, the young rancher had a gentle manner and Gwen warmed to it instantly. She was low in spirits and needed friendship.

She was a New Jersey girl, the youngest of the four children of W. W. "Billy" Grant, a successful construction engineer. She was educated at Shipley and at Smith, with a year out at sixteen to travel the world with her family. Billy Grant was eager for his youngsters to see the beauty and misery of the world at first hand. Gwen was inspired; and immediately after she graduated from Smith with an arts degree, she applied for a welfare job among the natives in the Virgin Islands.

A two-year assignment was offered, but Gwen's fiancé, John DeGroot Rawson, said he would not wait two years for her. She turned down the job and, in her words, "leaped into matrimony." Three children were not enough to soothe the basic imcompatibility between a man who could not settle in any job and a woman who wanted a man of action and dedication like her father. In the end, she decided to fend for herself.

It was not that easy. During her time at the dude ranch, she sickened with pneumonia and she grew steadily weaker when she was moved to a town hospital. Depressed with the hopelessness of her situation, she lacked the spirit to fight her illness. Larry was only a "new" friend then and she did not look to him for rescue, not at first. But day after day he brought the children to visit their mother in the hospital. He kept them washed and fed and read them bedtime stories. One small gesture touched her most of all: he plaited Jenny's pigtails every day and tied them with fresh ribbons.

On the way out of Gwen's hospital room one afternoon Mellon paused. He left the children at the door and walked back to her bedside. "Come on, get well," he said. "It means a great deal to me." From that moment on Gwen never doubted that she would regain her health.

If Larry had marriage plans then, he did not announce them. He did not have time. Japan bombed Pearl Harbor and he at once applied for enlistment in the Navy. For weeks and weeks he waited, but no word came. Peggy Mellon knew of her brother's impatience to get into the war. She was in Washington then with her husband, Tommy Hitchcock, the ten-goal polo player and flier who was organizing air transport for the European theater. At Peggy's intervention, Hitchcock got his brother-in-law the promise of a job with the Organization of Strategic Services (OSS) and Larry raced off to Washington.

"If you want to do something for me while I'm away," he told Gwen, "learn to be a good cowgirl."

The OSS welcomed Larry chiefly because of his talents as a linguist. He had spoken perfect French since boyhood and had picked up Italian, Spanish, Portuguese, and a fair proficiency in several other languages since. But the spy chiefs did not seem to want him in a great hurry. Told he would be called at any time, he purchased a watercolor set to occupy himself in his hotel room while he waited for the telephone to ring. He was even afraid to go out for meals. Several weeks passed before his assignment came through: Madrid.

In his three years of undercover work in Portugal, Spain, and Switzerland, Larry now claims that he did "nothing spectacular." He spied on German ships using the neutral ports, and along the borders of France and Germany, his job was to make contact with Underground leaders handling the escape of shot-down Allied fliers. He admits that he crossed behind enemy lines, but does not elaborate. "The work was secret then and I suppose it still is," he says.

Back home in Arizona, he continued his courtship with Gwen and finally proposed. "Surely you don't want me with three children," she parried. "I wouldn't take you without them," he said.

Gwen tackled her new role as a rancher's wife eagerly, although she had some tenderfoot troubles. She climbed out of bed at dawn every day to cook breakfast for the cowboys. The fire in the wood stove was harder and harder to start until one day it would not start at all. The cowboys watched her struggling with the tinder for a while; then, because they liked her, they announced: "Gwenny, you ain't dumped the ashes." Another time she had trouble milking the family cow, much to the delight of some visitors. A cowhand sidled past and whispered: "You're on the wrong side of the cow!"

However, Larry seemed to have lost some of his enthusiasm for raising cattle and Gwen felt it must be because the ranch had prospered equally well without him during his time in Europe. It became less of a personal challenge for him. He was more housebound now and that worried him, too. A last relic of his pre-war days of utter independence was the duffel bag he kept packed at his bedside. This disappeared after a few months when Gwen remarked jokingly, "You had better get rid of that. It makes me nervous."

They lived at first in a small house built on the ranch at the insistence of the elder Mellons. Then when Larry bought a new spread, the Fort Rock Ranch near Seligman, they equipped it with a spacious, modern homestead and put in a swimming pool. They needed the extra living space. Apart from Gwens' children, Larry was seeing more of his son Billy, and there was a stream of visitors from the east. At times Larry himself felt a little like a visitor.

"I had become a domesticated cowboy, a dude, and that spoiled the whole thing," he said later. As an afterthought, he added, "You can't ranch from a big house. It just doesn't seem like ranching."

Once again he grew restless and undecided about the future. Sometimes his mood sought strange outlets. When the Mellons were in New York on a brief vacation, Larimer phoned his wife. "I'm at the Berlitz School," he said. "Shall I learn Hebrew or Arabic?" After taking a cram course in Arabic, he arranged for a Syrian to come out to Arizona to help him perfect the language.

Unexpectedly the tutor brought along his wife and three children. They were not the ranching type. The man wore his Chesterfield coat and Homburg hat on the short walk between the bunkhouse and the main home. His wife did not venture out much because she was frightened of the deer in the area. She did like Gwen Mellon's big house, however. "If it was only in Brooklyn," she sighed.

When the family returned to Brooklyn, Mellon found that the only literature in Arabic that had been left for him to translate into English was, of all things, the Gospel of St. Luke. One part of the narrative gave him pause: the verses where Jesus discusses eternal life with a wealthy man. The man assures Jesus he has always obeyed the Commandments and wonders what else he has to do to guarantee entrance to Heaven. Jeus tells him to sell all his possessions and give the money to the poor. The rich man is obviously not prepared to make this sacrifice and Jesus reflects on the virtual impossibility of his ever getting into Heaven. "It is easier for a camel to go through the eye of a needle than for a rich man to enter the Kingdom of God," says Jesus.

Although he was not a regular churchgoer, Larry has complete faith in God and he believes in the teachings of the Gospels. His admiration for Jesus is very great. It was not hard for him to identify with the rich man—with the ranches and trust fund income, his personal worth approached two million dollars—and he thought about Jesus' message long after he had finished the translation of Luke.

Mellon was primed, emotionally and morally, for a change in his way of life, and the start of the transition can be traced to a night in November, 1947, when he returned home after a day roving across Fort Rock.

He sat in the living room and thumbed through a copy of *Life* magazine to a picture of an elderly man sitting on a log in the jungle with two antelopes standing at his side.

Life's caption to this picture of Dr. Albert Schweitzer at home described him as the "greatest man in the world." Mellon called his wife and together they read the story of the renowned theologian, philosopher, musician, and physician who went to Lambaréné in the wilderness of French Equatorial Africa to conduct a hospital for the natives.

Ironically, two days later Mellon received a letter from his brother Matthew in which the name Schweitzer came up in a mention of Matthew's studies of Bach. The jungle doctor was also the world's leading authority on Bach and the best interpreter of his music.

"My interest was really aroused then," Mellon recalls. "Gee, I thought, here is this man with four degrees and all sorts of other distinctions living with the natives in the jungle. To my recollection I was not immediately moved to follow his example or anything like that. But a week or two later an old school friend was visiting the ranch and I was telling him about Dr. Schweitzer as we were driving along in the car.

" 'You've got it bad,' he said. I asked him what he meant and he said, 'You'll try something similar to Dr. Schweitzer.' He felt that I had already made up my mind, but it actually was his comment that made me think for the first time of trying it."

Gwen Mellon's memory of the events leading up to what was to become a firm decision was much the same, although she did not know of the conversation in the car. She was considerably stunned when her thirty-seven-year-old ranch-boss husband sat her down and announced, "I want to go to medical school."

He had thought it all out, he said. He wanted to practice

medicine in the Schweitzer way. Against the opportunity to do this, such drawbacks as his age and his lack of the premedical academic training seemed minor.

Gwen heard him out. Then she said her piece: "You're right, Larry, we don't want to sit around here and look at those damn cows for the rest of our life!"

DRIVING THROUGH the timeless dark of Haiti, Mellon had completely transported himself back to his Arizona days and his conversation was injected with cowboy gee's and goshes.

But then his headlights picked out a desolate cluster of huts in a hungry wash by the road and he came back to present reality. He remembered his advancing middle age and the job that still faced him. Thinking back again on his sudden resolve to become a doctor, he got a little mad.

"It burns me up sometimes to think that I spent five years at medical school," he has said. "I could have been here five years earlier. A doctor has no special magic for a place like this. An intelligent layman could diagnose ninety per cent of the cases of sickness. Food, drugs, and bandages—that's what most of them need. The greater want goes beyond medicine and it can be filled by a variety of men. An agronomist can offer as much here as a doctor. In fact, any man of goodwill can be of service. As I get older, I see all this specialization as too much. Down here you realize it is not so important. What is important is goodwill."

It was true that Mellon had enough skills at thirty-seven

to donate himself immediately to a primitive land. But he had been so impressed by Schweitzer's philosophy and example that he could think of nothing he wanted more than to become a Schweitzer disciple.

He had sent a letter to Lambaréné introducing himself and explaining his decision, then dispatched a friend to seek first-hand advice from Schweitzer. Mellon himself had to stay in Arizona to sell the ranch. The friend turned out to be a hypochondriac; mosquitoes chased him away from Lambaréné before Schweitzer had a chance to talk to him. The great doctor must have been convinced of Mellon's earnestness, however, for in March, 1948, the rancher received a tightly written longhand letter in French from Schweitzer. It covered many pages and told Mellon exactly what he wanted to know.

Though he warned that a medical course would not be easy for a man approaching forty, Schweitzer said he was confident Mellon would get through if he tackled it full time. It might help if he followed a few suggested short cuts. While anatomy and physiology were vital, he need study only as much zoology and botany as was required to pass the examinations. If Mellon intended to practice in a remote area, he should have a thorough knowledge of surgery, certainly the know-how to conduct everyday operations. Similarly, clinical medicine was of tremendous importance, and since he might have to be his own pharmacist, he ought to pay special attention to this field, too. Skip detailed courses in tropical diseases, advised Schweitzer, because there was no better way to learn about those than to be on the spot—for instance, by visiting Lambaréné. "And more than anything else," wrote the wily old doctor, "don't try to pass your exams brilliantly. Be satisfied by simply sneaking through honorably. And don't pick a pretentious thesis for your medical degree. Take an easy subject which will not require lengthy research . . . just what is needed to wangle the degree."

Discussing a place for Mellon to practice, Schweitzer felt that nationalism was too strong a force in South America and humiliating conditions might be imposed on a foreign doctor. The best place might be in a colony, working as a physician with an American mission station.

"Independence is of the foremost importance if one wants to do something worthwhile and do it well," wrote Schweitzer. "You must resign yourself to many sacrifices, but try to avoid, as much as possible, sacrificing your independence. Here I am leading a very hard existence in many ways, but I find the strength to lead it because I keep my independence. I could not have done it otherwise."

This was one Schweitzer lesson Mellon was never to forget. Virtually, it was the secret of the success of Lambaréné. Another piece of advice he did not heed. He had an idea that the Amazon area offered the best opportunity for a jungle hospital and Schweitzer's doubts about South America did nothing to shake it loose. After his ranch properties were sold, he booked passage for the whole family on a freighter bound for Peru, intending then to travel over the Andes and investigate the jungles of the Amazon headwaters.

It was, according to Gwen Mellon, a terrible trip. The rainy season had closed in the country, but Mellon paid out enough to persuade a taxi driver in Lima to risk his life on the mountain roads and take the family prospecting for a hospital sight.

Indians, they found, were surprisingly few and far between

along the upper reaches of the Amazon. More negative, for Mellon's purposes, they were bursting with good health. He wanted his hospital to fill a maximum need. Such a need obviously did not exist here.

Ten weeks later, the family sailed for New Orleans, where Mellon applied for admission to the medical school at Tulane. Gwen, who wanted to work side by side with her husband, also applied.

Dean Max Lapham was skeptical of Larimer's chances of lasting the distance and he successfully dissuaded Gwen from trying it as well. "I'll stand down," said Gwen, "but if you don't see your way clear to take Larry, I think you'll be making a big mistake."

Lapham appeared startled at the edge in Gwen's voice—she was somewhat taken aback herself. "You're well over the usual age, Mr. Mellon," said the dean, "but we'll make an exception."

Gwen Mellon was to count the Tulane years as the toughest of their life. Between Larry's work and her own training as a laboratory technician, they rarely had time to sit down together for a cup of coffee. For five years—first while he completed pre-medical studies and then until he graduated—they did not go out socially. Gwen was interested to find the medical students as odd a group of personalities as "you'd find on a New York subway." In many ways her husband was the oddest. He had to study twice as hard as men nearly twenty years his junior to achieve the same results. And he had to battle unforeseen setbacks, like suffering a fit of squeamishness in anatomy class. It was a continual struggle for him to get average grades. His anxieties about passing gave him an ulcer.

There was no alternative to graduating. Schweitzer himself was watching Mellon's progress, and so, too, at closer range, was Schweitzer's good friend, Dr. Emory Ross. Ross, a retired missionary doctor, ran a New York fund-collecting office for the Albert Schweitzer fellowship and was also a minister of the Christian Church, Disciples of Christ, which the Mellons joined.

In 1949, still in his freshman year, Mellon flew up to New York one weekend to see Schweitzer who was visiting America briefly and was meeting people at a series of afternoon gatherings at Ross's Gramercy Park apartment. "I'll talk to you at two-thirty," Schweitzer promised Mellon as they shook hands at the door. Then the old doctor was engulfed in a mob of one hundred people.

Precisely at two-thirty, Mellon felt a tug on his sleeve and looked around into Schweitzer's animated face. "Now we'll have our little talk," he said.

They left the apartment and walked the streets of Greenwich Village for more than an hour. Schweitzer talked in French about Lambaréné, the problems of running a mission-type hospital, the need for more research on leprosy. He was so engrossed that Mellon had to stop and start him at street lights and guide him through traffic. At one point Mellon spotted a bright piece of jewelry on the sidewalk. With a cry of discovery, he picked it up and held it out in his hand for Schweitzer to see. The doctor kept on talking medicine, his eyes straight ahead. Mellon blushed like a boy and thrust the jewelry away into his pocket. He had learned something about single-mindedness.

Before the two men parted that day they arranged for Mellon to visit Lambaréné in the summer of 1951. In May of that year, Schweitzer cabled his protégé, suggesting he delay the visit because Schweitzer himself had to go to Europe. Since the Mellons had already farmed out the children and since it was the only time they had available, they went anyway. They traveled by way of the giant Firestone plantation in Liberia to study sleeping sickness, malaria, and leprosy. Down south they were stuck for three days at Port Gentil, waiting for a boat up the Ogooué River. They stopped at the modern French hospital there.

"We are not so intrigued with Schweitzer as you foreigners," a French physician told them one night. "You people go to Lambaréné but nowhere else in French Africa. I suppose part of our reaction is jealousy. On the other hand, we feel it is unfair. Schweitzer does not deserve fame for his medical work. He is a good doctor, but his hospital has received more glory than it is worth."

Mellon was a little unprepared for the native village atmosphere of Schweitzer's hospital—surprised, like everyone else, at all the fires outside where members of the family cooked for kin who were patients. But he was expertly instructed in tropical medicine and he did notice that the hospital was packed, whereas the spick-and-span French hospital down the river was almost empty.

On the return trip to the United States, the Mellons visited Schweitzer at his European home in Gunsbach, and Mellon told him of the French doctor's remarks.

"What he says is true," said Schweitzer. "I do not deserve my fame and it hurts me to have it. But what can I do about it?"

Contact with Schweitzer had developed in Mellon a quality of humility and self-effacement. He was able to submerge quickly his day-to-day worries and feelings because they seemed so puny in the light of the service he was equipping himself to perform.

Once, in a gesture of appreciation for Gwen's dedication to his cause, Mellon bought her a racy black Jaguar automobile. Gwen was working as a research assistant in a Tulane laboratory then and students ribbed her about toiling for wages when she had the means to drive a "Jag." Upset by this, she would not use the car again. Mellon himself drove the sports car until it was sold, giving his wife his own aged Ford. Only Gwen knew how Larry must have winced every time he climbed out of the Jaguar cockpit at Tulane and sensed the raised eyebrows of his fellow students.

Mellon's wealth was known, of course, but there was rare evidence of it at Tulane. During his senior year, a young resident, Dr. Henry K. Miller, asked Mellon if he was acquainted with a foundation that would give Miller fifteen hundred dollars to pay the return air fares of a Japanese student who wanted to train at Tulane. Mellon suggested that Miller write to a certain group in New York "and mention my name." By return mail, Miller got his fifteen hundred dollars. Not until much later and then only by accident did Miller learn that his friend had telephoned the New York foundation, promising to send a check for the money if they would advance it immediately to Miller.

For his senior year Mellon had to prepare a thesis. Noting Schweitzer's advice not to pick too complicated a subject, he decided to investigate and write about tropical ulcers. This time he wanted the whole family along on his field trip so he searched for a place reasonably near to New Orleans.

In the summer of 1952, the Mellons loaded on to a boat a

four-wheel-drive truck and camping equipment and sailed for Haiti.

They by-passed the swank hotels of Pétionville, up there on the hillside overlooking steaming, swarming Port-au-Prince, and plunged into the back country. By visiting villages and scattered wayside medical clinics, Mellon was able to gather excellent material for his thesis. He was also seeing at close quarters the suffering of Haiti. Though deeply saddened, he felt a growing excitement because somewhere here must be the place for his hospital. Later, in Port-au-Prince, an American engineer heard of Mellon's plans and suggested the Artibonite Valley, a great wedge of blighted land narrowing from Saint Marc and Gonaïves on the coast to the abrupt mountains of Haiti's backbone.

"The valley was a paradise once," he said. "Now all you can see is mesquite and cactus. And the people are living like animals—diseased, starving, dying. They have no clothes and they live in mud huts. It's like being in the middle of Africa."

An irrigation system was being planned for the valley, said the engineer, and if it ever came to anything peasants would pour into the valley by the thousand. Even now the area was overcrowded and desperately short of doctors.

Mellon drove ninety miles north over rough roads to see the valley for himself. It was truly in woeful condition. He called at a clinic in mid-valley to talk to the local Haitian doctor. The doctor had gone, deserted his post. It was then that Mellon was sure he had found the place of "maximum need."

All that was necessary to start his operation was official permission. He sought this immediately from President Paul E.

Magloire. Mellon told the president he wanted to build a hospital in the Artibonite Valley with a staff of his own choosing. It would not cost the government a cent; he just required land and he was ready to pay for it. In a generous mood Magloire replied that Mellon could have a small piece of land without cost for as long as he kept his hospital going. Standard Fruit was closing down its plantations and headquarters at Deschapelles, he said. Mellon could build there and have the use of some of the houses for his staff.

The terms were better than Mellon had dared hope; his only regret was that, counting his residency, he faced another three years of preparation. Resolutely he put out of his mind the bounding challenge of the future and immersed himself again in his studies.

It was left to Gwen Mellon to discover how history had set the scene for their mission to the Artibonite Valley, to see what had gone wrong since the warrior Dessalines had driven out the last of the Frenchmen and proclaimed Haitian independence on January 1, 1804. In those days, the Artibonite Valley, like all Haiti, was a tropical garden, and the Artibonite River forging through it was shaded with mahogany forests. Now the valley was devastated and the river an open brown wound. What had gone wrong?

The seeds of ruin had been sown unwittingly by the idealistic mulatto Pétion, who, in 1807, assumed command of the south of Haiti after Dessalines was murdered. Pétion wanted to sweeten the lives of his people, black and mulatto alike, so he sliced up for homesteaders the vast private plantations and great tracts of land that had been state-owned under Dessalines. The slices were too thin. Instead of farms, Pétion was creating peasant holdings. They were extremely fertile, however, and the Negroes, relaxing after their fight for freedom, were able to grow sufficient food for sustenance with little effort. The common attitude shied away from competitive cropping and trading, tending rather to self-containment. Pétion did not permit forced labor; besides, his laws were lax and his taxes low. It was no wonder the people called Pétion "petit père"—and no wonder that thousands defected from General Christophe's iron rule in the north of Haiti to enjoy the free and easy life in the south.

By 1820 Haiti had ceased to be a divided land. Christophe had avoided assassination by committing suicide. Pétion was dead. Another southern mulatto, Boyer, was in control of the young republic; he presided with the same gentle touch as his predecessor. Boyer finished parceling out the land to his half million citizens, and families who missed out on the giveaway simply went off into the back country and squatted in the sections that seemed thinly populated. Mud huts mushroomed all over the landscape. French plantation houses, water canals, mills, and roads, mostly gutted by the years of revolution, crumbled away.

Haiti had commenced its long slide into the dust as scarcely more than a land of peasants, its wealth in the hands of the few thousands of mulattoes who conducted commerce in the cities. Formerly rich exports of sugar, indigo, cocoa, and cotton fell to a trickle. Coffee became the main cash crop but only because it grew wild. No country abroad showed enough interest in the welfare of the republic to offer assured markets for its tropical produce. There was scant incentive to push hard at anything. Other countries did not even recognize Haiti's independence for fifty years or more. It was an outcast in the world.

And within Haiti itself, the peasants were outcasts, their circumstances permitting them to see no other way of life. Generation followed generation, planting the same ground with corn or beans until the land itself sickened and soured. When they wanted fuel or more land for crops, they cut down trees, slowly denuding the hills and letting the rains wash the rootless soil into the valleys and rivers.

They traded food and primitive wares such as cooking pots and straw hats at the country markets and in the towns. Men did the buying and selling at first; but as later Haitian presidents sent out press gangs to kidnap men for the army, the women took over the marketing role. They were more aggressive than the men anyway and better collectors of gossip. Their language was a French patois, Creole, the dialect of a people who had no knowledge of French grammar or spelling and simply spoke French by sound.

The day-by-day battle to survive was brutal, but it never defeated the peasants or drove them into savagery. Voodoo remained as their comfort and discipline. It brought self-expression and dignity into their narrow lives. For the peasants, it was not a matter of having faith in voodoo. It was a voodoo world, just as it was in Mother Africa, and the peasants were proud and willing members. The handiwork of the voodoo gods was everywhere, evident not only in a rainstorm but in more devious manifestations such as an individual's good or bad fortune. The overlap between the supernatural and the natural, the spiritual and the physical, was inviolate.

Voodoo gods, or *loas,* whom the peasants associated with the Catholic saints and angels, were not purely ethereal.

They would materialize—to give advice or to condemn, or sometimes simply for tomfoolery—by entering the body and mind of the worshipper. A peasant would be a peasant no longer; for a brief period, he might even be Loco, the god with healing powers. With the right sort of sacrifice and frenzied preparation, any avid worshipper could be possessed by his favorite *loa.*

There were hundreds of *loas,* each with a specific range of authority and a distinct personality. Roughly speaking, *loas* of the Rada family performed good deeds and the Petro family gods worked evil. Even good gods had human weaknesses. Some were vain, others quick-tempered, others downright lascivious. All this added to the theatrics of a voodoo ceremony, many of which lasted through Saturday night and into Sunday. Every ceremony was different, depending on the imagination of the participants and the creative impulses of the drummers and dancers. Riotous *loas* could turn the show into an orgy. *Clairin,* raw white rum, could have the same effect.

Although the Haitian peasants and the Negro slaves on the plantations of the American South had common ancestors, the fixedly primitive society of Haiti and its voodooism set the two groups far apart. Attempts to colonize freed American Negro slaves in Haiti failed utterly. An American named James Redpath tried it just before the Civil War. In his brochure he said the Haitian peasants were "of never-failing good nature, thoughtless of the morrow, polite and sociable, but without ambition."

Peasants in the Artibonite Valley, where Redpath aimed his migration, did aspire to owning more land. Otherwise, there was a tacit agreement that collective security depended on resisting change. Valley society was knit as tightly as a reed sleeping mat—one independent thread and the whole thing might unravel.

Redpath persuaded about twelve hundred adventurous Negroes to take the free passage to Saint Marc, where Nicholas Geffrard, then president of Haiti, promised to support them until they were given ownership of a piece of rich farm land.

While Redpath claimed that he had personally inspected the valley, his enthusiasm was more descriptive of the Artibonite of French colonial days. "Sugar cane grows the year around," he wrote, "and so fast and thick that by the time the laborer has cut over and exhausted a ten-acre field it is ready to be cut again." According to him the Artibonite could produce sugar enough to drive Louisiana out of every market in the world, tobacco enough to kill Virginia on the Liverpool Exchange, rice enough to bury Charleston. Corn? Drop a seed in the ground and up it would shoot, fifteen feet high. The valley bubbled with mineral springs and was cloaked with forest. As for Saint Marc, it was a health resort.

They arrived, faces shining in the Haitian sunlight, those twelve hundred Negroes from Boston. Yellow fever and typhoid decimated them in Saint Marc, and government officials stole their baggage. It was many months before a few blocks of land were doled out, and then the land was waterless. Some brave men persisted, but the Haitians so resented improvements like fences, fertilizer, water tanks, that they rustled stock from the newcomers and spoiled their crops. Very few black men from Boston stayed on to endure such treatment. Most escaped back to America.

After that, the routine of Haiti was not interrupted for many years. Peasants gouged what they could from the land, and politicians and mulatto traders in Port-au-Prince squeezed what they could from the peasants. A procession of greedy dictators passed through the presidential palace.

Inevitably, however, fear sent one of them berserk. In the early summer of 1915, President Guillaume Sam massacred two hundred citizens whom he thought were plotting against him. Port-au-Prince was horrified. A mob ferreted out Sam and tore him to pieces with their hands. A Negress was seen shredding the president's heart with her teeth.

The United States declared Haiti in a state of anarchy. Americans there were not safe, their investments were in jeopardy. Gunboats landed marines on Haitian soil and a nineteen-year occupation began.

Educated mulattoes were put in charge of the government. The grossly expensive army was disbanded and replaced by a doubly efficient small constabulary. Towns were electrified, telephones installed, roads built. Small industries were launched, cars and buses imported. Peasants were taxed less, and they saw doctors and schoolteachers for the first time in their lives.

The occupation rankled, nonetheless, and the pressure in Port-au-Prince to end it grew year by year. President Sténio Vincent, freely elected, had his chance for glory when Franklin Delano Roosevelt became President of the United States and gave Haiti back to the Haitians. But Vincent's first act was to amend the constitution to increase his powers. His successor, Élie Lescot, went even further.

Haiti was slipping backward. The roads were breaking up, the telephones would not work, industries were closing, graft was seeping back into government, the doctors and school-teachers were returning from the country.

Then an extraordinary thing happened.

A military junta chose as president Dumarsais Estimé, a Negro politician dedicated to improving the lot of the peasants. Within a few years, however, the jinx of the office was to corrupt him, too, and Magloire would take his turn. But before that happened Estimé justified his term as president by coaxing an initial six million dollars out of the U.S. Export-Import Bank to irrigate the Artibonite Valley and reclaim its land wastes. The loan was enlarged as the blueprints were finished and the total budget was boosted still more by American foreign aid money and Haitian government grants.

Peasants were skeptical when they heard of the grandiose plan for their valley. They would believe it, they said, when they saw it.

A young American agronomist named Charles B. Wiggin, Jr., assigned to Haiti by Point Four, tramped about the valley for weeks studying the soil and the land grading. He was awed by the task of repair but confident it could be done.

"The suddenness of the advance will prove bewildering," wrote Wiggin and the rest of the technical team who drew up the plans for the semi-autonomous *Organisme de Development de la Vallée de l'Artibonite* (ODVA). "Construction of the project will pave the way for increased agricultural production by means which have not been used since the French colonial days of the late 1700's."

And if this seemed to be taking a page from distant history, it was a good page. Technicians dusted off a copy of a report submitted to Paris by French engineers in 1777. The report recommended precise irrigation methods for the fertile valley floor to make it a true horn of plenty. Paris financed the project and soon the valley was pouring out torrents of sugar, indigo, cotton.

Now, the surplus food yields from the peasant farms were negligible. There was no irrigation, except on Standard Fruit's banana groves. The rest was a dreary landscape of salt flat, marshland, thornbush country, and limestone hills. Remaining woodland was fast being razed. Agriculture had not reached the wheel- and wooden-plow stage. Land was prepared with the hoe, seed was sown with the hoe, crops were harvested with the machete.

A large family on a seven-acre plot was lucky to make three hundred dollars a year. The family was also lucky to have seven acres. To stay alive, peasants had to hoe and plant every square inch of soil, back-breaking labor they faced on a cup of coffee and a biscuit for breakfast, a shot of rum at mid-morning, a roasted corn stick for lunch, and a bowl of rice or beans for supper. On a good night they would flavor the rice with a piece of pork. Meat was short because there was less than one animal per person in the valley. Many of these were pack horses, mules, and burros. Valley markets seemed busy, but the week's salable produce of the typical peasant woman was pitifully modest: perhaps some ochre and sweet potatoes. This would bring a total of thirty cents with which to buy a bottle of vegetable oil and a cake of soap. There was something tragically childlike about it.

Investigation by Wiggin and the other technicians showed that thousands had starved to death in the valley and disease was rampant. Yet on the plain itself, the peasants had only one hospital, a fifteen-bed clinic at Verrettes. Hospitals at Saint Marc and Gonaïves were inadequate for the townspeople, quite apart from the peasants. Doctors faced a hopeless task. They knew it and stayed away.

Life expectancy was not much beyond thirty, but since love making was a nightly routine the population increased steadily. The ODVA men could not create more land for the growing masses. Their job was to make the existing land produce a great deal more food. A dam would be built at Peligre, at the throat of the basin, to regulate the flow of the Artibonite River. Thirty miles downriver they would begin the crisscross of canals which would water almost the entire floor of the valley.

It was a fine plan and the ODVA went to work. Wiggin, in Panama hat and polished ankle boots, was the technical director. Target date to revitalize the valley was 1962, ten years in the future.

By then, ODVA hoped to have new roads down and rice mills, canning plants, cotton gins, sugar factories operating. The United Nations fish expert, Dr. S. Y. Lin, said the canals would be seeded with fish. That was it: the Artibonite was to become a rich valley of rice paddies and fishing streams. Town planners envisaged modern villages with grocery stores, restaurants, dry goods shops, beauty salons. Schools would be built to accommodate every child of the Artibonite.

Such was the promise of this gaunt valley when Larimer Mellon first arrived on the scene and Magloire gave him permission to go ahead with a hospital for Deschapelles. Rumor in Port-au-Prince had it that Mellon's plan was final proof that America intended to colonize the Artibonite.

The peasants did not have the cunning to think of this. They listened politely and nodded when they were told that one day their valley would be another Garden of Eden. But their eyes said "Show us."

5

BY 1955 the Artibonite Valley had become a place of action and high expectation. At the head of the river canyon, way up in the hills, the Peligre dam was completed. And down below, near where the river first started to curl and carve its way deeply across the plain, the walls were going up for the Hôpital Albert Schweitzer.

Fifteen million dollars and the lives of fifteen men was the cost of Peligre. A local engineer explained that the men "fell off things." Larceny by government grafters in Port-au-Prince had put the dam way over budget—merely a taste of things to come—but it was still worth every penny because it could save the valley from dying of thirst. One hundred billion gallons of clear mountain water swelled behind the sluice gates and backed into a lake that stretched to the border of the Dominican Republic. In the valley, American bulldozers gouged out the canals that would course this water through thick fields of rice and sugar, tomatoes and cucumbers.

Off by the sea, on the rising ground outside Saint Marc, the Mellons had moved into an old stucco house. From there they commuted to the construction site of the hospital about twenty-five miles away.

"It was the best summer I ever had," says Jennifer now. Then nineteen, she had gone down in June with her mother and brothers to help supervise the building. Mellon himself was completing his residency in New Orleans. He was due in Haiti with his son Billy in August.

Gwen and her family whitewashed the Saint Marc house, flushed out the bugs, rigged up a shower, then joined the Haitian laborers on the hospital job. They poured concrete, carted stone, and planted trees. The big Mellon house, low and winged, with a forty-foot living room opening through an entire wall of folding doors on to patio and garden, went up at the same time. It was immaculate. Its discreet elegance reflected Gwen's taste, and while it was the sort of house that would have looked well in Grosse Point, Michigan, it did not seem out of place in Haiti's backwoods. Judging by his bachelor days in Arizona, Larimer might just have settled for a converted *caille.*

A mulatto physician, jealous of the Mellon hospital, inspected the house and reported to his friends that it must be costing a hundred thousand dollars. "This is charity work done the American way," he muttered, "in twenty-four carat comfort."

A Catholic priest had a similar view about the hospital. "All stainless steel and no personality," he said.

Deschapelles was off one of the limestone roads that branched from Haiti's main trunk road between Port-au-Prince and Cap Haitien. The turnoff was easily missed altogether by visitors who did not see the small signboard tacked on to a tree trunk. From the tree, a Haitian contractor had rough-cut a road the half mile to the hospital free of charge. Peasant huts, some thatched and a few with iron roofs, lined this road which was already well traveled by long-striding, tireless native women who carried on their heads wares to sell at an open market adjacent to the near corner of the hospital grounds. An avenue of trees led into these grounds and to the settlement of stone bungalows, built by Standard Fruit, which housed the American irrigation engineers. The hospital took over several of these houses later, but for the time being the staff bunked in one of the wards. The ODVA had a clubhouse, a small swimming pool and an asphalt tennis court in this modern colony. The pool was used often, but the weather was usually too hot for tennis. In the court, peasants dried their corn.

A circular flagged courtyard fronted the main reception and out-patient wing of the hospital. Three more long, low-gabled pavilions, two at right angles and one parallel to the main, sided another courtyard in the middle of the complex. Covered walks led to a fifth pavilion on the river side. A cobbled stable yard, where peasants could shelter their tough little horses and burros, extended beyond the toilets at one end of the main wing. Later plans called for a "community center" pavilion for classrooms, sewing rooms, living quarters, even an ice cream shop.

Nothing was stinted. To the left of the front waiting room with its records department and pharmacy were bright, louvered wards for pediatric and surgical cases and an isolation ward for TB patients. On the right were the air-conditioned operating rooms, out-patient clinic, X-ray department, laboratory, and morgue. There were staff offices, a medical library, a cafeteria, a vast kitchen, bulk stores, a generating plant for electricity. The hospital had its own water supply, its own telephone system. A hundred-acre farm was acquired nearby to provide scarce protein foods like meat, milk, and eggs.

Initially it was to be a fifty-five-bed general hospital—no maternity cases—serving the broad area around Verrettes. Because of the special facilities, the hospital would take TB and ophthalmitis patients from all over Haiti.

The Mellons had set up the Grant Foundation, named after Gwen, in Pittsburgh to handle the operating expenses of the hospital. After a capital outlay of more than one and a half million dollars, an annual budget of close to two hundred thousand dollars was fixed for the hospital. This would take all of Larry Mellon's trust fund income, a sum which had been boosted by inheritance after his father died in 1949. While W.L. had held reservations about his son's projected new career, the old man knew it would have pleased Mary Taylor Mellon: she had died seven years earlier.

Although Mellon knew the hospital would not be self-supporting for many years, if ever, he wanted right from the start to get the peasants accustomed to paying for treatment. He was thinking ahead to the day when he would either be dead or his money exhausted. The hospital might then have to earn its own way. He fixed a fee of three gourdes—sixty cents—a clinic visit for local patients and four gourdes for people who came from outside the district. The in-patient fee of six dollars a day, which might well be the equivalent of a full month's earnings for a peasant, was based on the cost of an average funeral—about thirty dollars. If a peasant was willing to pay this to bury his dead, he should pay a similar amount to save a life. A minimum of five days' hospitalization would be needed after a major operation. This cost was calculated at six dollars a day.

Mellon smiled at his prices, knowing he would be lucky to collect a fraction of them. He also knew he would not be turning away anybody in his district. Nonetheless he would keep asking. If peasants wanted to settle their accounts with a sack of rice or a turkey, that was all right, too.

Staff recruitment had been another difficult problem. The offer of a comparatively small salary earned in a distant, disease-ridden valley was not exactly tempting. But eventually Mellon found five doctors, including a surgeon and a pediatrician, who were willing to sign eighteen-month contracts. Nurses were more plentiful. Already he had five Haitian nurses training in the States, perfecting their English and learning the latest hospital techniques. In addition, several American and Canadian nurses heard of the project and volunteered.

Miss Walborg L. Peterson, then executive assistant to the director of the Massachusetts Eye and Ear Infirmary, was the most distinguished recruit. "Miss Pete" had heard of the hospital from a friend of Peggy Hitchcock. She showed such keen interest that Mellon went to see her in Boston. They sized each other up quickly, Miss Pete finding the doctor "humble, sincere, enthusiastic."

"I can offer only myself," she told him, "but I want to do that." And so Mellon acquired, as his director of nurses, one of the best medical administrators in the United States.

While Larimer organized, Gwen fraternized. The only way to go further into the Haitian interior beyond the hospital was on horseback, and Gwen did so often to meet the peasants in the hills and to tell them of the hospital.

Some Americans working in the valley mistrusted the Negroes. They were nervous that a peasant, either on impulse or when hopped up with cheap rum, might run amok with a machete. Their imaginations ran riot at the sound of the voodoo drums throbbing across the valley every night. But a few white families—like the Mellons and the Wiggins—loved the atmosphere and assimilated eagerly. Gwen's small tribe could not get enough of it. They kept away from voodoo ceremonies and cockfights—the peasants considered these their special and exclusive property—but Saturday nights they were welcomed at the black man's thatched nightclub near Saint Marc. There, along with the peasants, they danced the *meringue* until dawn.

Soon after Mellon arrived in August the children reluctantly returned to school in America. But there was little time for the *meringue* now as Larimer and Gwen set about speeding up construction and importing equipment from New York. Mellon worked so unobtrusively that at first the people of Saint Marc had no idea who he was. Later one of the local men told the doctor that the people had decided he was there to escape the draft.

In a recurring bad dream suffered by Gwen at the time, she opened the doors of the splendid new hospital and nobody came for treatment. Actually, however, sick peasants started coming to Deschapelles months before the hospital was ready. Dr. Mellon treated the most serious cases as best he could. He even visited the sick in their huts, although he resolved that "house calls" would not be part of the hospital service. Because of the inaccessibility of many peasant settlements and his limited staff, such calls were totally impracticable. The hospital needed tough rules like this to survive; Mellon had to school himself to be as secretive as possible whenever he broke them.

"Larry wanted to help these people day to day, hand to hand, mouth to mouth," said Gwen. She was aware that he was feeling his way among the peasants, trying to be of service yet guarding against misplaced sentiment. One day he stopped his car by a peasant on the road. The man was in rags, the shreds of a shirt falling off his back, and his pants so tattered they were barely decent. Impulsively Mellon gave the man a gourde. It was accepted with bewilderment rather than thanks. Rags did not necessarily indicate a poor man, Mellon scolded himself as he drove off.

Early in 1956, Miss Pete arrived to organize her nursing staff; with trainees, it would number twenty. And soon afterward the doctors assembled. Already on the scene was Dr. Loren "Yank" Chandler, on his first sabbatical in twenty years from the University of California. Chandler had agreed to set up the surgical services at Deschapelles and perform the first operations, but he spent most of his time opening packing crates. Similar duties befell the husband-and-wife medical team of Harry and Burma Nordstrom and the rest of the professional staff.

Opening date for the hospital had to be set back several times. Peasant laborers had to be shown how to do the same simple jobs over and over again, causing endless delays. Delivery of materials was haphazard, and tons of cement were looted. Despite the purpose of the building operation, some workmen tried to make do with shoddy results. An electrician who put up the wrong gauge overhead wires did not confess his mistake for a year.

Although the finishing touches were still being applied during May, the staff decided to start the hospital functioning on June 26, Mellon's forty-sixth birthday, come what may. Nurses and doctors scrubbed the entire hospital, finished unpacking medicine and equipment, and set up the beds.

At six in the morning on June 26, Gwen Mellon took her place behind the registration desk as hospital personnel filed in for the first of a series of rehearsals. Mellon himself manned a post in the medical section of the clinic. Other doctors waited in the pediatric and surgical divisions.

During the next few days, as each member of the staff was given a thorough medical checkup, a simple routine was evolved. Patients from within the district who had their three gourdes for a first visit or two gourdes for a subsequent visit would be immediately "processed" at the front counter and assigned to the appropriate clinical department. Local patients without money would be told that they would be seen, but that they would have to go to the end of the queue. People from beyond the district would have to wait outside until a doctor inspected them and decided whether they were sick enough for emergency treatment.

Word spread through the district then that the Hôpital Albert Schweitzer was ready. Shortly before dawn on the morning after July 4, Gwen and Larry Mellon walked together on the foot track from their new house to fulfill a dream born in Arizona nearly nine years before.

"The beginnings are always difficult," Albert Schweitzer had written in a letter to the Mellons. "But you are courageous."

Courage they needed, the courage of a medical rescue team caught under siege in an advance army field hospital, with more and more wounded arriving by the minute and nowhere to put them. The peasants came in droves—fifty each clinic day, then a hundred, then two hundred, and three hundred. All the dread diseases were there at Mellon's front door. He and his men treated every one of them, but only the worst could be admitted. By doubling up in children's cots, the hospital accommodation was increased to seventy in-patients. More beds were put in the corridors. Still this was not sufficient. Peasants ravaged by venereal disease or wasting with pulmonary tuberculosis were dosed up, injected, given future appointments, and sent away the same day. Other outpatients came in with rheumatic fever, heart disease, malaria, whooping cough.

Back in the States, a physician liked to have at least an hour to "work up" a patient and perhaps arrange for consultations with specialists to confirm diagnosis.

At Deschapelles, with babies dying of tetanus and old men collapsing from starvation right there in the clinic, the doctors could not afford more than five or ten minutes for most patients. Consultation, however, was not such a problem. It was just a matter of calling down the hall: "Hey, Harry, come and have a look at this."

It was difficult, despite the use of interpreters, to get adequate case histories. The peasants answered *oui, oui,* to everything and their description of symptoms was vague. With persistence, though, the doctors could gather some horrifying information.

Dr. Alexander Earle, one of the pediatricians, examining the infection around the navel of a baby with tetanus, asked the mother how the cord was cut.

"Machete," said the mother.

"Did you keep the navel clean?" asked Earle.

"We rubbed it with dung," said the mother. "Our baby will be fertile."

Earle came across many voodoo superstitions that directly affected his work and he made a note of them for an article for the *Pediatrics* journal. "Cow's milk is too strong for babies who have just been weaned," he wrote. "Goat's milk is no good for babies of any age. (Goat's milk is used as an aphrodisiac among the adults.) Bananas and oranges are too cold for small children and will also excite the intestinal worms commonly present and give the children a stomach-ache and make them swell up. A newly delivered mother must not get her feet wet and a person with jaundice must not cross a river. (Doctors cannot treat jaundice as it is best treated by 'tea leaves.') If a frog urinates in your eye, it will cause blindness; the people almost panic at the sight of a frog. All windows and doors must be tightly closed at night to keep out the evil spirits. (There are usually eight to twelve people sleeping in an eight- by twelve-foot room; one or more of them may have active tuberculosis.)"

In the surgical ward, Harry Nordstrom took a tough line against voodoo medicine. An old man limped into his clinic with an enormous leg ulcer. Nordstrom gave him a penicillin injection and told him to come back in four days. Dutifully the man returned. His ulcer wound, however, was covered with a red powder, a supposed magic cure.

"M'sieur," said the doctor, "either you accept our treatment and only our treatment, or don't come back."

From that day on, the old man converted to white man's medicine.

Another time a man was brought in with bruises, cuts, and small circular burns covering his back. He explained that he had bruised his back when he fell out of a mango tree. A local witch doctor had made a number of cuts over the bruises and then drawn out the evil spirits with the rim of a hot glass.

Several peasants arrived with cords bound about various parts of their body. A woman with a severe headache had a tight string about her neck "so the pain won't travel down." Another with stomach pains had a cord cutting into her waist and a second around her chest to confine the pain.

Yet the doctors were reluctant to condemn all voodoo medicine. The native herb specialists sometimes satisfied their patients. Even hospital employees swore by the Haitian common cold cure: one put dried red flowers from the chulak tree in a jug, poured in boiling water, and covered it for four minutes. By this time, the liquid would be jet black. A squeeze of lime was added and it turned bright red. The patient then drank the concoction. Asthma sufferers burned these same red flowers and inhaled the smoke.

"We must remember that these leaf doctors have borne most of the burden of country medicine since French colonial days," Mellon said in a discussion on the issue one night. "Sure, they mistreat patients, but so do all doctors sometimes. The *bocors* do know how to treat malaria and average cuts and pains. And they understand the psychiatric problems here better than we do. I've seen a broken leg perfectly set by a *bocor*. They recommend bed rest for tubercular patients, and this is okay."

Nevertheless Mellon was pleased when the famous *bocor* of Deschapelles, Monsieur Paul, came to him and said he was closing down his business in deference to the superior work done at the hospital. Subsequently, Monsieur Paul became a landlord, built several simple houses in the village and rented out rooms to hospital out-patients. He still retained his reputation in witchcraft, and one of the rare times he used it was when Gwen Mellon begged him to intervene in the case of a peasant woman friend who believed she was dying under an evil spell. The curse surrounded her hut and the woman refused to move outside for fear she would drop dead. Marching fiercely into the imaginary accursed circle, Monsieur Paul broke the spell and made the woman immune from further devilish design.

Peculiar, often vile peasant sicknesses, both of body and of mind, taxed the knowledge of the doctors to the limit. They went back to their textbooks time after time. One surgeon opened the belly of a man, inspected certain organs, and summoned a faint smile. "Phew," he muttered. "I don't know what it is, but it is the worst case of it I ever saw."

Though many ailments indeed required expert and detailed treatment, many more were aggravations caused by privation, especially lack of food. A high school student could arrive at a quicker diagnosis in such cases than a doctor. The obvious treatment, rest and nourishment, would have been sound, but the doctors were prone to seek a more sophisticated reason for lethargy, dizziness, stomach pains, wasting, and skin breakdown.

Doctors don't diagnose what they don't think of, Mellon often reminded himself in those early months. He tried to think of everything, but he was frequently disappointed at the inadequacy of his medical knowledge and that of his colleagues. His long ago idea of medicine as the magic cure-all science did not stand up to the supreme test of making the grossly neglected bodies of Haitian peasants whole again. There was no miracle drug for chronic starvation.

In its absence, Miss Peterson told her nurses to use what she called TLC—tender loving care—and this performed as many miracles at Deschapelles as any antibiotic. Two patients who proved the medicinal value of TLC were numbers 488 and 489, Sylvanie Datilus and her seventeen-month-old daughter, Marie-Rose.

Mellon found them in the clinic waiting room one morning in an advanced stage of "starvation and hopelessness." The emaciated mother sat on a bench, with the almost lifeless little girl falling out of her lap. Sylvanie mumbled her story to the doctor. She was twenty years old and had recently buried her two other children who had died of hunger. She was not married, her father and mother were both dead, and she had been living with friends in a hut a bare quarter mile from the hospital. The "friends"—Mellon has quoted the word in his dossier notes—had given the mother and daughter a place to sleep, but no food.

Down in the medical ward, Mellon spoon-fed Sylvanie until she fell into a deep sleep. With Marie-Rose, however, it was not so easy. Dr. Earle rated her chances of survival as extremely poor. He began intravenous feeding, but the only response in twenty-four hours was a feeble cry. All the second morning Earle sat at the baby's bedside. She was weakening and seemed beyond help.

"If we lose the baby, we lose the mother too," said Mellon. Sylvanie was taking nourishment only under repeated urging. She looked at Mellon with the blank eyes of a fast-ebbing spirit.

Earle looked again at his own tiny, pitiful patient and

called for a blood transfusion and more intravenous feeding. Cécile Déjoie, one of the Haitian nurses Mellon had sent to the United States for training, kept watch during the night. The little girl's breathing improved, and when she awakened on the third day Cécile coaxed her into taking a few spoons of puréed vegetable and liver.

For the next week, Marie-Rose passed through a series of crises. Several times she came close to death. She was not alone in the fight. Cécile Déjoie and Nurse Marie Grimond were always there with their medicines and their Pablum, applesauce, and milk.

So Marie-Rose was brought back to life, and the sight of the baby's smile worked the same wonder on her mother. Six weeks after their admission, Gwen Mellon took them home. They wore new, starched clothes and carried a large carton of cornmeal, rice, beans, and powdered milk. Sylvanie no longer despaired about the future. Soon indeed she was to start as a permanent employee of the Hôpital Albert Schweitzer.

This case confirmed Mellon in his policy of urgent, individual attention for every peasant who entered his hospital. He wanted his doctors to share the suffering, not let their familiarity with it make them detached. The common medical phrase, "clinical material," angered him when he heard it applied to the Haitians. Schweitzer had told him once that compassion was indispensable in a good doctor. Now he saw the full worth of this quality. It was easy to fend off the heartbreaking scenes at Deschapelles with a barrier of hardness, but Mellon would not allow himself this defense. Rather, he felt a sense of privilege that he had somehow found his way to a place where he could be so exultingly human. Never was a task too menial, a duty too unsavory. He emptied bed pans, dressed the dead, and wiped vomit from the floor.

One day an old man, filthy and suppurating, lay sunken with hunger on the lawn outside. Lifting him to his feet, Mellon put his arm around the bony shoulders and walked him slowly into the hospital. The old man smelled badly, but Mellon did not turn his head away, nor did he look about for a washbasin to cleanse himself once he had eased his patient into a wheelchair.

There was the sad afternoon when a little girl came to Deschapelles with a cancer that had gnawed at her mouth and nose. She stood there in distress, looking up at Mellon, her face half pretty and half raw flesh. The doctor picked up the little girl in his arms and carried her to his house. He sat her on a divan on the front porch, and then went to the music stand to play the flute for her. After an hour Mellon carried the peasant girl back to the hospital and put her in a clean bed. He smoothed the hair back from her forehead and bent close to whisper, *"Au revoir, chérie."*

In the morning she was dead.

IT WAS AN EXHAUSTED, shocked, and frustrated medical team that toiled through those first weeks and months at Mellon's new hospital in Haiti.

Their life was measured in clinic days—Mondays, Wednesdays and Fridays. They kept hoping that each clinic day would get better. Instead, they got progressively worse. Every time there was a bigger invasion of sick people to be repelled with injections, drugs, and bandages, and every time more and more of the diseased, dying, lame and infirm had to be taken in.

On the face of it, all seemed very orderly. District peasants registered at the desk with Jerome Jean-Baptiste or Gwen Mellon, paid money if they had it, and were directed to one of the doctors. Each of the doctors, the physician and the pediatrician and the surgeon, had consulting offices in the main front hospital wing, just beyond the reception room. Patients sat on wooden planks outside these offices and waited for their names to be called. There was no pushing, arguing, or queue jumping. Newcomers were stunned by this great *blanc* palace of medicine. The people who had been there before contemplated the Haitian paintings and the framed pictures of Lambaréné on the walls, or they sat in silent agony.

It was inside the consulting rooms that the doctors, nurses, and interpreters came face to face with the truly sad and terrible procession of clinic days.

The Haitians entered with absolute trust in their eyes, expecting to be healed. They did not know what they were asking. The hypodermic needle, they thought, cured everything. One doctor had a patient with cancer. Told that he would need a big operation, blood transfusions, and the rest of it, the peasant was unperturbed. "Okay, doctor," he said. "But when do I get my *pici-pici?*"

In the medical clinic, Mellon alone saw seventy of these trusting patients on some days. One after the other, into his office came people with tuberculosis, typhoid, malaria, malnutrition, intestinal parasites, peptic ulcers, hypertension, gonorrhea, diabetes, heart disease.

Some had two or three of these ailments at once. Others had mysterious aches and pains that they simply described as *"mal en bas coeur,"* which meant discomfort beneath the heart and which could have been any one of a dozen different sicknesses. Was it gastritis, or an ulcer, or worms, or had this patient merely been taking aspirin on an empty stomach?

Mellon studied the dossiers kept on each patient for notes about any previous sickness. He inspected the flesh beneath the fingernails for paleness and signs of anemia, measured blood pressure, listened to the heartbeat. All the time he asked questions: diarrhea? lost weight? difficulty in breathing? fever? appetite? If he was lucky, he could match up two danger signals in a few minutes of consultation.

High blood pressure and a dizzy feeling might mean hypertension. He could prescribe good drugs for this complaint. Diarrhea and a stomachache suggested amoeba and he could treat this with sulphur tablets. But a third symptom here might be the vomiting of blood, meaning perhaps an ulcer. Mellon had to be careful to get all the information. Any shade of doubt and he would order chest X-rays, blood tests, and other laboratory analyses.

Rarely did the peasants come up with a precise symptom that led Mellon instantly to the nature of the disease. One woman talked about her lethargy and excessive thirst. As an afterthought, she said that ants were eating her urine. This observation may never have been made before in the history of modern medicine, yet obviously the woman's urine had a very high sugar content; she was suffering from diabetes. Mellon used insulin to control diabetes, penicillin against venereal disease (if caught early), and injections and tablets against malaria.

But there was no really satisfactory way to treat a man like twenty-one-year-old Joseph Success. His stomach had been swollen for a year, he told Mellon, and now his leg was swelling up. Under questioning, he revealed that his older brother had died of a coughing sickness. Joseph Success, it turned out, had chronic pulmonary tuberculosis, a common disease in the valley. Because there were only a few beds in the isolation ward and these were already filled, Mellon had to send the man home with drugs.

"I have lectured the patient on the necessity for faithfulness in taking his medication. We'll see," Mellon noted in the dossier on this patient.

Sometimes, in cases of leukemia and cerebral hemorrhage, Mellon had to write "prognosis hopeless" on dossiers. Because there was no chronic disease hospital in Haiti, the people were given sedatives and sent home to die. Beds at Deschapelles were occupied by potentially curable patients.

Nor did Haiti have a hospital for the mentally ill. The doctors at the Hôpital Albert Schweitzer had to admit some of the deranged peasants and try to treat them medically. Not infrequently a man would go berserk in the middle of the night, crying like a wounded animal and running about the wards until the night staff could corner and tie him down. Insane people were mostly cared for by their families, although a few were cast out to roam the country. Along the road a few miles from Deschapelles, a crazy old woman, who lived in a lean-to under a bush, greeted passers-by by poking a stick at them and lifting her skirts. A lunatic man wandered the northern roads, raving, his legs almost eaten away with ulcers.

Part of Mellon's job was to screen the out-of-district patients on the steps outside the hospital, separating the seriously sick from those who could wait to see the doctor in their own area. This screening was essential to keep numbers down to a manageable level, but it was still the most difficult job at Deschapelles and Mellon hated it. Each clinic morning he saw twenty or thirty people and made snap diagnoses. The peasants wailed and moaned and prostrated themselves on the ground; they were desperate to gain admission to the clinic.

Mellon's assistant in the screening was Jerome Jean-Baptiste, who was much better than the doctor at detecting trickery. Jerome knew that some rich people from Port-au-Prince left their cars down the road, changed into old clothes, and hired peasants to carry them to the hospital. Others produced borrowed birth certificates to "prove" they were in-district. One mulatto girl from the town of Gonaïves paid a local peasant to pose as her husband so that she could get treatment for gonorrhea. At the last moment, however, her pride forced her to admit the deception.

Although Mellon worried over missing some one on the steps who was really sick, he seemed to have a sixth sense about where to find true suffering. One day he glimpsed a man slumped against the wall at the back of the shelter, apparently sleeping. Mellon noticed the rapid rise and fall of the Haitian's chest. Suddenly, the doctor was off through the crowd. He felt the man's forehead and hands. They were cold with impending shock. Back through the throng Mellon went, returning a few seconds later with a wheelchair. As he pushed the man through the clinic toward the X-ray room, he was giving quiet, urgent instructions to the nurses. First an X-ray, then an electrocardiogram, then to the ward for oxygen, and an injection of digitalis. By this time, the man was rolling his eyes and breathing fast, his shoulders rising and falling to lift his rib cage. When Mellon read the X-ray, he saw why. The heart was huge, flabby, failing. Another few hours without treatment and the man would have been dead.

Mellon himself was spared the second screening session—the selection of child patients. This was done by Gwen Mellon and the pediatrician. These were the most heartrending cases: children who were broken and wasted and lame. Not many of the youngsters were healthy enough to be refused; Haitian parents did not take their children to the hospital just because they sucked their thumbs.

There were sights that have been etched in Gwen Mellon's memory for all time. One was Marie Oraceus. At birth she might have been called one of God's children, but that thought would not have occurred to anyone now that she was five. From her deathly appearance, Gwen could tell that she was crawling inside with worms. There was no flesh on the girl, just the outline of her skeleton under paper-thin skin. The skin itself was hot and dry and hideously mottled with pink and black patches. She leaned silently against her mother's shoulder, lifeless except for a faint heartbeat that seemed about to stop altogether.

Gwen Mellon demanded an explanation. Tearfully the mother said she and her man had had a fight. Out of spite the man had taken Marie with him and then left her with a family who did not want her. Marie had been cast into the corner of a hut, given a few scraps of food and an occasional bowl of water, and allowed to rot. For weeks the mother had searched for her daughter. At last she had found her only that morning and brought her straight to the hospital. Marie was admitted for intravenous feeding. At least she died without having to eat another mouthful of dust.

On clinic days Gwen spent most of her time interpreting for the pediatricians. Parents took a seat in the aluminum chair before the doctor's desk and submitted their children for examination while they answered Gwen's questions about symptoms. In this role, her tired handsome face was lighted now and then by fleeting smiles. She sat erect, a slender woman in a simple flowered dress and thong sandals. She had a lightly tanned skin, soft brown hair flecked with white, and blue eyes. Her only adornments were a solitaire diamond ring and black-rimmed glasses often pushed up into her hair.

The pediatric clinic looked out upon a pleasant cobbled

patio planted with trees and cooled by a fountain. Inside, however, the scene was devastating.

The healthiest children had just stomach pains, lack of appetite, and nightmares caused by worm infection. They were given sulphur tablets and food supplements like fish powder, powdered milk, and vitamins. For added safety, cough medicine and anti-malarial pills were put on the list. In addition to these mild cases, the sicknesses progressed up the scale to pneumonia, diphtheria, typhoid, meningitis. Then, too, there were the babies near death with chronic malnutrition, and there were endless cases of lethal tetanus caused by unclean childbirth and the voodoo rite of rubbing dung or pot black on infant navels.

On the first few clinic days Gwen had been shaken by the extreme cases, but she expected the children to improve as parents brought them for treatment in the early stages of sickness. Months passed, however, without change. She cajoled, insisted, became angry, yet not too many parents understood what was expected of them.

On Mondays, Wednesdays, and Fridays, morale throughout the hospital was low everywhere. The third department, the surgical clinic, was jammed with women patients choked inside with advanced venereal disease, with women shot through with cancer of the cervix, with men with tumors and twisted limbs and hydroceles and hernias.

People with inoperable cancers were gently told of their condition and sent away with pain pills. But if there was one chance in a hundred that a swelling or tumor might not be malignant, the patients were taken in for examination and complete laboratory checks.

There were a thousand different ways in which the intricate machinery of the human body could become befouled. At Deschapelles, the doctors would think they had seen them all and then still another would turn up.

A "general" surgeon in the States usually indicated a visceral–internal organs–surgeon. In Haiti, however, every manner of radical cancer surgery was required of a general surgeon. He had to do skin graftings, hysterectomies, to correct typhoid perforations, to perform neuro-surgery and orthopedic operations. If he had never done a particular operation, he would go ahead anyway with surgical charts open at his side.

Among the milder cases in the surgical clinic was a young peasant woman with part of her bottom lip missing; it had been bitten off. This was how some Haitian women dealt with rivals for a man's affection: they disfigured them for life. In the clinic the wound was dressed and the woman was given penicillin.

A much more serious case was that of an eight-year-old girl with such severe burns over much of her body that there was barely enough good skin left for grafting. She had suffered convulsions and fallen into the fire, according to her parents. Such ghastly injuries, however, were not unusual. Actually the girl may have been exposed to fire purposely during a voodoo ceremony. Students of the cult said the fiendish spirits in black magic rites demanded human sacrifice and torture. Such ceremonies, however, had supposedly been discontinued long ago.

Although the doctors treated hundreds of voodooists, even high priests, their mystical world remained closed to the *blancs*. Yet everyone at Deschapelles felt the nearness of voodoo. Like the dire reality of clinic days, this bizarre presence became part of their lives.

On most nights the sound of drums—pagan, insistent—worked on the imagination until it seemed to come closer and closer. White people at the hospital climbed out of their beds to check door locks. Few if any wandered out into the darkness to seek out the drums.

Gwen Mellon, however, did so one night to record the rhythm at close range. When she saw fires in a clearing, she crept through the fields and hid in the bushes. Glistening black bodies crouched over drums and peasants moved about in curious ceremony. With the drums pounding in her ears and her heart pounding in her chest, she was both frightened to death and bitterly ashamed of herself. After making the recordings, she left her hiding place and went home. Actually neither she nor her husband intended to interfere with the voodoo beliefs of the peasants. Voodoo is the one true culture the Haitians can call their own, according to Gwen.

Around this same time, Protestant missionaries in Haiti, scorning their Catholic colleagues because they had "made peace" with voodoo instead of fighting it, claimed that twenty per cent of the population had now been converted to Protestantism. These peasants had renounced voodoo forever, said the missionaries. And some of them put Haitians through a kind of confessional in which they had to say why they no longer believed in their native religion.

Gwen Mellon doubted the missionaries' claim. Because the Haitians' big ceremonies came around Christmas time and at Lent, she maintained that they were held in defiance of Christianity.

While thousands of inhabitants of the valley had certainly

made the transition, others professed Protestantism simply to please the *blancs* at Deschapelles. Often a mother who described herself as Protestant would bring to the hospital a tetanus baby with pot black on its stomach.

Then, too, a "Protestant" houseboy for an American family was gossiping one day about a Haitian neighbor who wanted to leave his shrewish wife. The husband was stopped when he became convinced his wife had put a spell on his food. If he left her he thought he himself would sicken and die.

"Come now," said the Americans, noticing the boy's gravity, "we thought you didn't believe in voodoo any more."

"I don't," said the boy. "But if a woman can get at a man through his food, then I suppose it must have some power."

This dualism was apparent every Sunday morning when many of the Haitians attended Mass at the hospital's Catholic chapel, then went home to hold a special service for their guardian voodoo saint. The bowl of peanuts and corn left in the corner of many a *caille* was not put there for human consumption but to feed a hungry spirit, while the perpetually burning lamp was supposed to guide his way. And fifty dollars buried in a tin was a poor family's guarantee that, when hardship became unbearable, they could pay a witch doctor to conduct a full ceremony for St. James, the Protector.

Deschapelles once had a nightwatchman who whistled over and over the same monotonous few bars of a dirge as he made his rounds. The rumor spread that he was a zombie, one of the walking dead, reclaimed from his grave. For many nights Haitian nurses and nurses' aides refused to go home unescorted. They did not get over their fright until the man was produced in daylight and shown to be normal.

Peasants used to carry sticks at night in case they met a zombie. Few doubted their existence. If one man's field produced a superior crop to his neighbor's because his land was more fertile, the neighbor gave no credit to the fertility of the soil. He was sure that the other man had poor, dumb zombies tilling and watering his crop in the dead of the night.

Because of their tradition of superstition and ceremonial witchcraft, Haitians decided that Mellon's medicine was as much a matter of rite as of science. Whether they needed them or not, they liked injections, the stethoscope check, pills, and the little white rendezvous slip that set another appointment. To them the routine was part of the curative process. Instructions on how to use medication were frequently confused; the peasants lacked the slightest concept of how medicine worked.

Once, for example, an injured man had to have one of his eyes dressed; he was given pills to swallow and ointment to put on the eye. He returned to the clinic in a mess. He had put the pills under his bandage and tried to dissolve them into his eye by pouring water on his dressing. In doing so, he had rubbed the ointment all over his face.

Another patient required a blood transfusion. Mellon sent for the relatives to come and have their blood tested to see if they would be suitable donors. Blood supply was always a persistent problem. Doctors liked to keep their own blood for emergencies; it was best to wait three months between pint donations. For this reason, the family and friends of patients were usually appealed to for blood. This particular patient had a large family circle, but each member was found to be too anemic to give blood. Instead of a hemoglobin count of at least twelve, these people had a count as low as four. The doctor kept asking for stronger, healthier relatives. Finally, some of the clan came and said, "We've got one for you now, Doctor." Mellon followed them outside. They had brought the family horse.

Shrewder peasants played on such ignorance to set themselves up as specialists in white man's medicine. Their blunders sent several patients to the hospital. One man had stomach cramps after attending a "clinic" in a nearby village. He was a victim of the oldest quack trick in the world. A white-coated mountebank had sold him a cure-all tonic; its main ingredient was muddy river water.

The most cunning of the quacks capitalized on the peasants' blind faith in the magic of the *pici-pici.* He went from door to door with a can of condensed milk and a hypodermic needle. For a gourde he shot the milk into the buttocks of gullible peasants, producing ugly ulcers.

Such abortive attempts to copy *blanc* methods of healing showed, however, that Mellon was gaining ground over voodoo medicine. But in spite of this, and in spite of the crush of patients at the hospital, the peasants were still loath to break with their old ways. A little boy, for example, once misunderstood a question about symptoms. He thought the *blanc* wanted to know why he had come to the hospital. Before the mother could stop him, the youngster announced, "Because mama didn't have enough money to take me to a witch doctor."

A Haitian who had worked for a voodoo priest and knew him to be a charlatan asked the hospital staff for help in coaxing his wife to have her rheumatism treated at Deschapelles.

He had tried, he said, but his wife's parents had demanded that she go to a priest instead. She was adamant and only went to the hospital after her money was gone and the priest had failed.

Mellon noticed that many peasant men had an ugly inch-long scar in the center of their chests. He suspected some kind of fetishism. Perhaps a gash had been made in the chest and fitted with a piece of animal's horn as a good luck charm; then the flesh had grown over the horn. But whenever Mellon asked the cause of these scars, the peasants always insisted that somebody had thrown a stone at them.

Turning the question around one day, he said to a scarred peasant, "I suppose somebody threw a stone at you?"

"No," said the Haitian, "I got hurt when I fell out of a tree."

In such ways the peasants kept discouraging *blanc* intrusion into the world of voodoo.

7

WITHIN MONTHS of the opening of the hospital, Larry Mellon feared that he might have taken on more than he could handle.

"I had no idea of the real situation," he said. "Think of it. We started service with four cribs in our pediatric department. Soon fifty were not enough. I thought I could get by with one pediatrician, one internist, one surgeon, and one general physician. Twice that number would have been overworked."

At the root of the trouble was Haiti's lack of any public health service. The Deschapelles hospital was jammed with people suffering from preventable diseases. Mellon immediately started to immunize the children and to teach parents about the need for this. To no avail, however. The parents were just too ignorant to understand that disease could be avoided, or at least checked if caught at the outset.

Mellon could not fight this ignorance adequately without fighting the illiteracy of the valley peasantry. This seemed entirely beyond his resources. Nor could he institute sweeping public health programs. For one thing, that was the government's province. For another, he had neither the staff nor the money for it.

Money! That was another factor he had underestimated. Two hundred thousand dollars a year would not pay the bills. Fees from the peasants did not even cover the one thousand dollars' worth of tuberculosis drugs prescribed each month.

In this crisis, Mellon forced the pace harder and harder. On the three clinic days the medical staff often worked from six in the morning until ten at night. On the other four days there were emergency clinic cases, in-patient checks, immunization sessions, and a full schedule of minor and major operations to perform. Mellon himself had little taste for surgery, but he had to assist in many operations.

The handful of doctors shared night call and almost never slept six hours straight. Sometimes operations went on until three in the morning. The workers in the laboratory and pharmacy were also on call day and night. Nurses were so hard pressed that local women had to be given rush training as nurses' aides.

Desperate, Mellon sought more doctors from the United States. And even though his hospital was largely unknown and he was offering only five hundred dollars a month, some Americans applied. Eagerly he put them under contract.

One physician, an alcoholic, returned to the bottle at Deschapelles to keep up his courage. He became addicted again and nobody could stop him. When he set fire to his bungalow in a drunken stupor, Mellon, losing patience, paid the man his money due under the contract and ordered him out.

Another doctor, expecting to find a backwoods glamor to

Dr. Mellon

Robert Phillips, Washington, D.C.

Gwen Mellon and a small patient

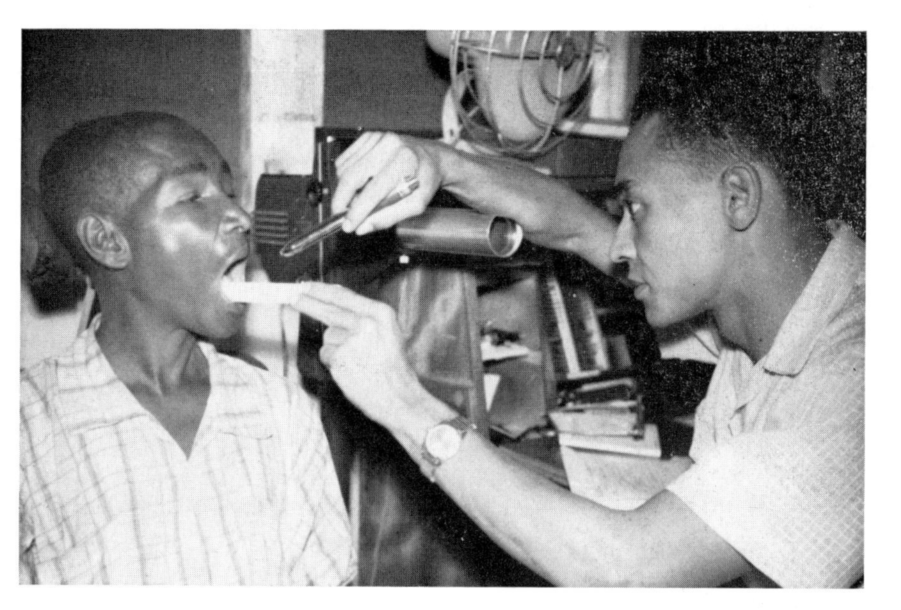

Dr. Gérard Fréderique, the hospital's brilliant ophthalmologist, dedicated to his Haitian people

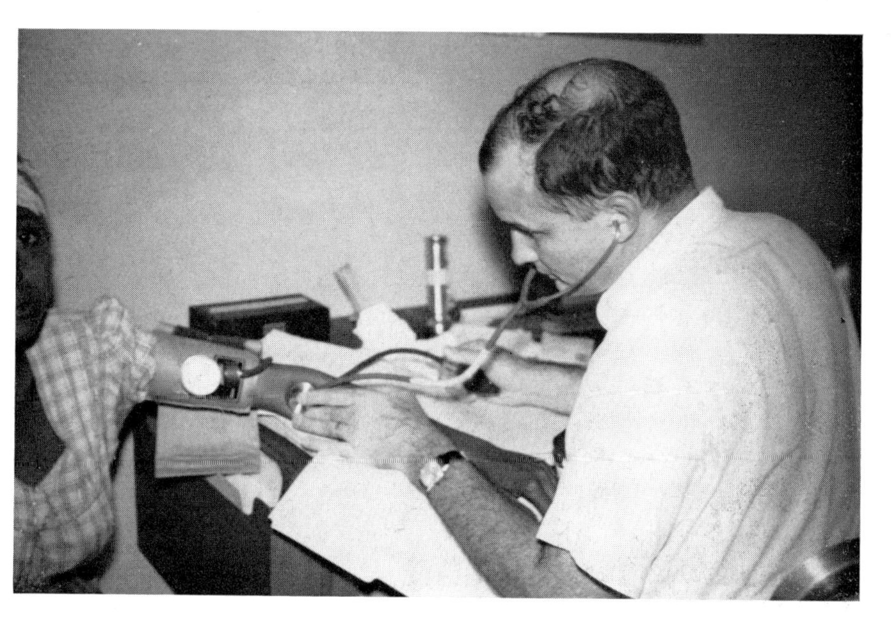

Dr. Robert Hollister, the missionary's son from New Berne, North Carolina

Dr. Réné St. Léger . . . "a man becomes a monster"

A peasant child awaits treatment for chronic worm infection

Outside the hospital, a man cradles his woman, who is in a near state of collapse with pulmonary tuberculosis

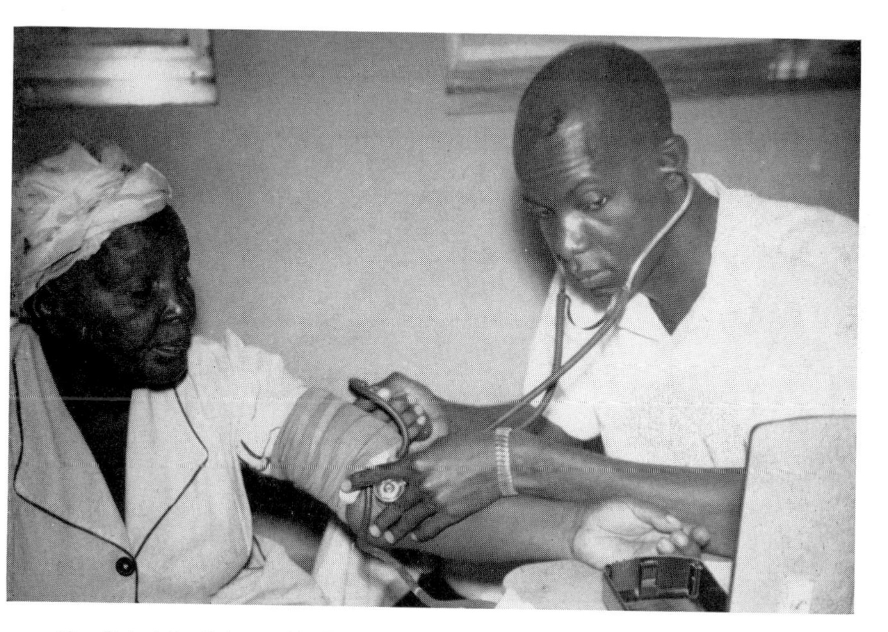

Dr. Réné St. Léger checks the blood pressure of a peasant woman during medical clinic

Dr. Harold May, the hospital's chief surgeon

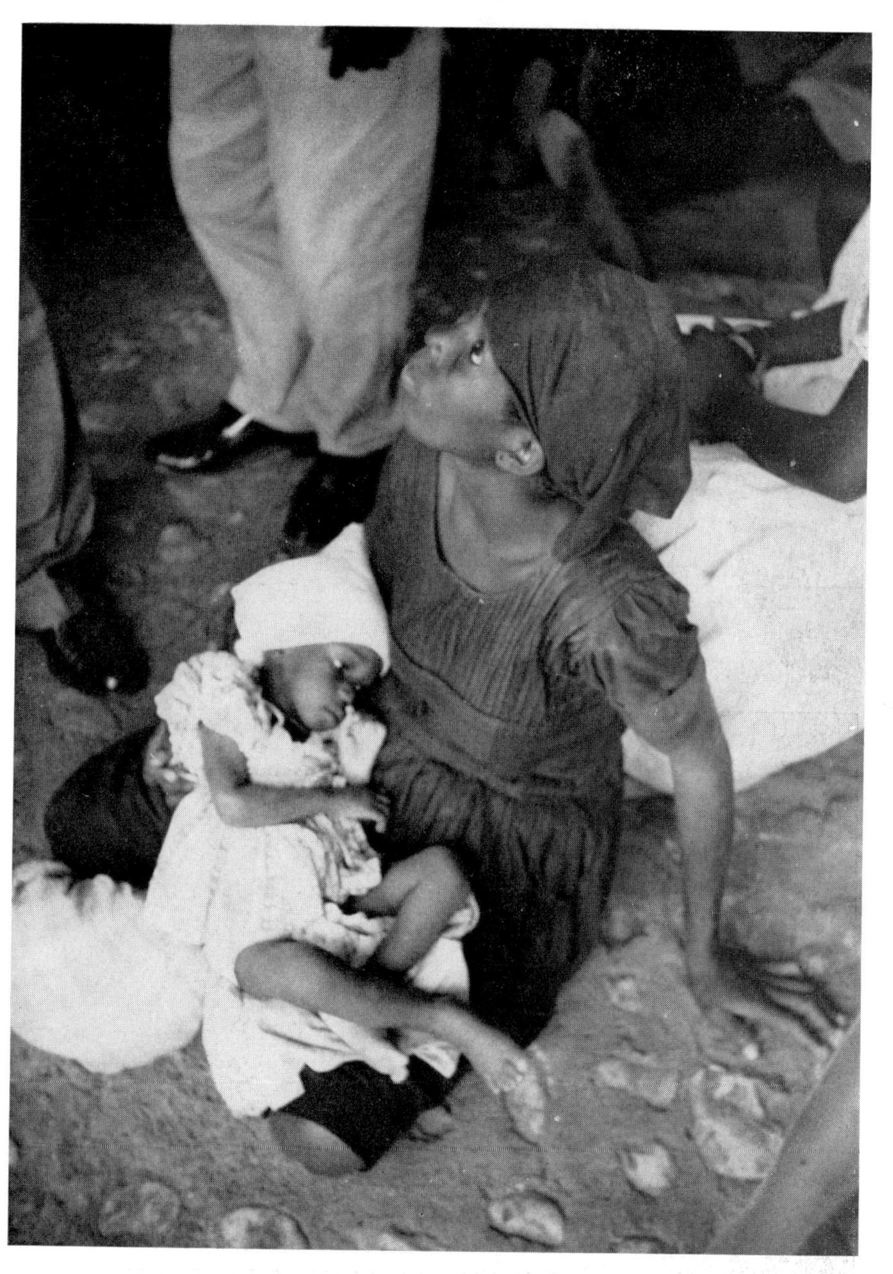

On the cobbled courtyard outside the hospital, a peasant mother and daughter wait to be seen by doctors

Patients for the hospital

Clinic day at the hospital . . . Peasants are ferried across the Artibonite River to keep their *rendezvous*

service in Haiti, was stupefied at the mountain of work. He complained that it was unjust. Mellon paid him for the full term and sent him away. His replacement arrived in high spirits, promising to stay forever. A few days later, Mellon received a note saying that he, too, was fed up and had left for Port-au-Prince. Another man got off the plane in the capital, took one look at the slums near the airport, and straightway booked a return flight on the next plane out.

Then Mellon himself cracked up. He suffered severe heart palpitations which his colleagues blamed on tension and exhaustion. Mellon would not accept this diagnosis; he could not. He insisted that his sickness stemmed from the ten or twelve cups of strong Haitian coffee he drank every day. Abstaining from coffee, he went shakily back to work.

Gwen collapsed next. Her back gave way under the strain; she was flown to New York for a disc operation.

This was the low point. Mellon now had two choices: either to give up or to cling to what he had and to embark on a long-range program to improve this part of Haiti, a task that would not be finished in his lifetime. The first alternative did not occur to him; a rough plan of action for the second was already forming in his mind.

Brochures describing the work of the hospital would be prepared and sent to individuals and organizations in the States, appealing for gifts of money and medicines. Future applicants for medical staff jobs would be screened in New York. On the public health side, more intensive instruction in hygienic living would be given at the hospital. Properly balanced diets would be recommended; classes in midwifery held; simple movies were to be prepared on the cause and dangers of tetanus and malnutrition.

These things were done with varying success.

The tetanus movie was so effective that after repeated showings at the hospital and in local villages it was rerun on television in Port-au-Prince. Its message was no less needed there.

Dozens of expectant mothers attended the midwifery lessons, watching nurses demonstrate with a plastic doll how to deliver a baby. These women were given kits containing a razor blade, a tie for the cord, and a large piece of sterilized brown paper on which to put the tiny child. Thereafter many fathers came to Deschapelles, with both the new-born infant and the placenta wrapped in the brown paper, to ask a doctor to cut and tie the cord. Though they had not fully understood the lesson about neonatal tetanus, cutting the cord appeared important. So they decided to let the *blancs* take care of it.

Stubbornly, however, cases of tetanus and malnutrition continued to rise at the hospital. These two diseases still killed off at least half the new-born babies in the valley. It was the old story of a closed mind on sickness prevention. No matter how often the peasants were told that lack of protein, for instance, caused the wasting and swelling of their children, they remained convinced that the babies would have been stricken whatever they had eaten.

More hopefully, additional funds, medicines, and other gifts started to arrive when the rest of the Mellon clan heard of Larry's budget problems and when pamphlets about the hospital were circulated. "Our most pressing need is your concern," said one of these appeals. "Please make your checks payable to the Grant Foundation, 525 William Penn Place, Pittsburgh 19, Pennsylvania."

Mellon's luck with his staff began to change about the same time. His own health had improved remarkably—at least, he said it had. Gwen was back, completely healed now except that she was forbidden horseback riding. Miss Pete was getting excellent nurses by warning off the timid ones. By letter she cautioned nurse applicants about the heat and isolation, and added that they would need vaccinations against tetanus, typhoid, diphtheria, and polio. If the girls still came, Miss Pete usually could guarantee that they would fulfill their contract of eighteen months or two years.

If, after a few weeks, the new nurses went to Miss Pete in tears, she always knew what to say. "Give it a little time. Soon you'll feel part of all this and won't want to leave." Almost invariably it turned out that way.

Notable among the new doctors was Dorrien Venn, a surgeon from Johannesburg who had worked with Schweitzer, and Harold May. The latter, a young Bostonian, traveled to Haiti in January, 1957, to see if a missionary doctor was needed in the land. He got no further than Deschapelles. Mellon implored him to stay. May explained that he could remain six months at the most. He was going blind and would need corneal transplants on both eyes.

May recovered by awsome faith in "Christ's guidance." After six months for the operation and convalescence in New York, he returned to Haiti. He later served an eighteen-month residency at Massachusetts General Hospital, but in 1960, he became Mellon's permanent chief of surgery.

Another dedicated doctor arriving at Deschapelles during the first year was Florence "Skeets" Marshall. She shared a pediatric practice at Hempstead, Long Island, with Dr. Robert McGovern. Out of pure altruism, these two offered to work a yearly rotation—the one in the States earning the money for two. It was an arduous system, but the Marshall-McGovern team kept to their bargain.

Work pressure eased as Mellon gradually built up his staff to ten doctors, including a dentist, ophthalmologist, anesthesiologist, and a second-string surgeon, physician, and pediatrician. Many of these men paid their own fares and served short terms. Thus scores of doctors came and went through Deschapelles. The hospital in Haiti was soon being talked about in medical circles around the world. It was a Lambaréné with all modern conveniences. Europeans and Filipinos applied for positions as well as Americans and Canadians. And many specialists offered their talents for brief periods. A regular shuttle of orthopedic surgeons, neuro-surgeons, and gynecologists was established. The comparatively few permanent doctors welcomed the turnover in staff because it enabled them to keep up with the latest techniques. The peasants would have been mightily impressed if they had known about the standard of medical practice they were offered. An operation costing a thousand dollars in New York was free to them.

The benefit, however, went both ways.

Young doctors sought experience in handling extreme cases; they gained more in a month in Haiti than during a year in America. Mostly they returned home with added confidence and stature, lectured once or twice on the Hôpital Albert Schweitzer, and that was the end of their Deschapelles connection.

A few, however, were no longer content to tackle the medical problems of Suburbia or to play the petty politics of American hospitals. They went into research or looked for another post in a faraway place. Renée Bergner, a pediatrician from New York, took her lawyer husband Arthur to see the work at Deschapelles. After three months of observation and labor, he went home to study medicine himself at New York Medical College.

Doctors were often religiously inspired, earnestly seeking to please God by devoting themselves to a term of mission service. But: "Some of these men go to Haiti more for their own good than for the good of the people," said a former Mennonite nurse who held second thoughts about the depth of purely spiritual motivation.

Deschapelles, then, did not evolve as a pocket of saintliness, unique on earth. The white community was a tight group of Protestants, Catholics, one or two agnostics, an occasional Jew, and some who did not declare their faith. They were human beings, however, and therefore a degree of intolerance, selfishness, jealousy, and personal sniping existed among them. Haiti was not their home and most of them did not intend to stay for long. Their true heartfelt associations were back in Winnipeg or Cleveland. The majority offered their sweat and skills but not their complete selves.

Mellon preferred the wholly dedicated person, people like Harold May and Miss Pete, but these were of a rare breed. In any event his staff of men and women usually worked hard and well, often brilliantly.

One example of a less than saintlike man who has proved his value at Mellon's hospital is Andrew Gallagher. The hospital was a self-contained piece of civilization; its life depended on the three big diesel motors providing electricity, air-conditioning, and refrigeration. When the maintenance engineer quit in 1957, Mellon hunted carefully for a replacement and finally selected a ship's engineer with a reputation for keeping engines turning through hell and high water. Gallagher was doubtful at first because he hated hospitals "even to visit." Besides, he thought that he would be living in a grass hut. But he went anyway, saying that if Mellon was not satisfied with his work to just say so and he, Gallagher, would leave. Shortly after he arrived, he faced a crisis caused by the incompetence of a predecessor. The electricity lines into Wards One and Two gave out, blowing the main fuse. Within three hours, Gallagher had thrown in an emergency line, proving to Mellon that he was the right man for the job.

"It's a matter of staying on the ball and not relying too much on the Haitians," Gallagher, a scrawny man who still speaks with a decided New Jersey accent, says now. "Those guys would always be asleep at the switch. They're not like Americans; they don't want to improve themselves. Take an American type like me. I was just a cab driver and then one day I said to myself, 'Here you are sitting around, getting a big ass and nothing in the head. You don't know if the pistons in this cab are going up and down or around and around.' Well, I started to read about mechanics and then I studied engineering at night. A Haitian would never do anything like that. When I take on a new boy at Deschapelles, he spends fifty cents out of his first pay envelope for a pair of dark glasses. After putting these on, he holds a book in his hand so I won't think he's asleep. And what's the book he's holding? It's not even about engineering. It's about the Jehovah Witnesses!"

In many ways Gallagher is the antithesis of the missionary type people expect to find in bush hospitals. Yet the Haitians quickly learned to like and respect him. Through nightlong operations, the surgeons knew that he was always somewhere around making sure that the air-conditioning unit was functioning one hundred per cent. And when the first big open house party for Haitians and *blancs* was held at Deschapelles, Andy Gallagher was its guiding spirit. Mellon has needed him almost as much for his rough and ready spontaneity as for his talent with engines.

Through the years the doctor was to find this quality of goodness in the most unlikely men. A New Yorker named David L. Baird started sending twenty-dollar checks to the Hôpital Albert Schweitzer each month. They were so regular that a Baird Fund was set up to provide out-patients with the truck fare home and a ration of food. On a visit to New York, Mellon himself called on Baird in his Wall Street office to thank him personally and to explain how the money was being used. It was the middle of winter, but Baird's windows were wide open and his secretaries wore overcoats. The man himself was rasping into one of five telephones, apparently closing a deal to buy a collection of jewels from some place in Harlem. After he hung up, Mellon introduced himself and talked about the hospital. Baird listened without comment, then called a secretary to find out how much money he had given over the past few years. It was six hundred and twenty-five dollars.

"I'll send the money each year now instead of monthly," he said. "It's the better way."

Writing Mellon a check for the same sum, he ushered him out the door. A month later, the usual small check from Baird arrived in the mail, and they have continued to do so every month after that.

Even more memorable was Mellon's encounter with Charlie Ponte, a tough-talking Italian who runs a music store in mid-town Manhattan. Still wearing a worn suit from his Arizona days, Mellon walked into Ponte's store one morning to buy an oboe reed. Ponte sized up Mellon, gave a grunt, and cut a few dollars off the price. He did the same when the doctor brought in a flute and a clarinet for repairs. The last time Mellon was not carrying cash and asked if a check drawn on an out-of-town bank was all right. Ponte asked what bank. His down-at-the-heels customer explained that it was the Mellon bank in Pittsburgh, which should be satisfactory because he was one of the Mellons associated with the bank.

"I should blow my brains out!" Ponte exploded. "I've been giving you the cheapest prices. Why didn't you tell me you were rich?"

This outburst did not do justice to the real Charlie Ponte either. One day another shopper who was obviously rich wanted to buy an expensive saxophone. As part of the deal, he asked for a few basic lessons. Ponte, a former clarinet player with Paul Whiteman's band, took him upstairs. A half hour later Ponte had made up his mind. The man would never learn the saxophone so the storekeeper refused to sell the instrument to him.

How the temperamental Italian could make a profit was a mystery to Mellon, but he liked his unique approach to business. The two became firm friends. After that, Ponte visited Deschapelles for a brief spell each winter to help Mellon teach interested peasants how to play musical instruments. Ponte and his host also played duets during lunch in the staff cafeteria and again at Mellon's house before dinner. Mellon, a capable musician on several instruments, usually spent the cocktail hour at his music stand.

One evening Mellon walked Ponte two miles into the hills to serenade a peasant girl about to have a baby. Outside her hut, they seated themselves on a knoll and started to play, Mellon on accordion and Ponte on clarinet. As the melody of "I'll See You in My Dreams" spread through the Haitian hills, a group of twenty or thirty peasants formed to listen. Ponte suddenly stopped blowing.

"What are we doing here, for Pete's sake?" he demanded.

"Charles," said Mellon, "do you know of anyone in the world who would appreciate our music more?"

Ponte was thoughtful for a minute. "No," he said, lifting the clarinet to his lips and resuming the melody.

Ponte gave away dozens of musical instruments to the peasants of Haiti. Word of this reached Manhattan and friends wanted to know his angle.

"So, what angle?" he growled. "I make a little here and I chisel a little there, so I can give away a few instruments. You know why? In New York I am just another guy trying to make a dollar. Down there in Haiti I give away instruments and offer music lessons for free and I feel like a millionaire." At this point Ponte paused and his round face lit up. "Boy, am I a sucker!" he said.

Deschapelles also brought out what Charles Ponte called the sucker-streak in a curious collection of people. A shady New York nightclub operator sent big checks to the hospital. A mid-western doctor named Tom White told Mellon he did not want to continue his service at Deschapelles, yet he stayed on and on without accepting a dime in pay. A Pittsburgh dentist, Dr. John B. Nelson, though ultraconservative and against welfare in principle, arrived at the hospital with a gift of dental equipment worth four thousand dollars. "I'm sick of the attitude back home where you're invited to a party and the host wonders when you're going to invite him back," said Nelson.

Mellon was heartened by all these men, and by the Haitians, too, who showed that virtues like kindliness and compassion were not dead. One such Haitian was Gus Ménager who ran the hospital farm and kept Deschapelles self-supporting in meat and vegetables and most other foods. Ménager could not bear to see suffering; he was always bringing or sending sick people to the hospital. Most were poverty-stricken, so Ménager paid their bills as well. There was also Monsieur Delinois, the successful coffee trader of Petite Rivière. This brown, bespectacled little man built and supported an old folks' home out of his own pocket.

"Whenever I'm discouraged," said Mellon, "I just drive on over to Petite Rivière."

To cap it all, Larimer's globe-trotting brother Matthew succumbed.

Matthew Mellon had been idling away the years, strolling the deck of his yacht, dabbling in archaeology, building an estate in Jamaica, and villas in Europe. When someone once suggested that he must be pleased about Larry's medical work, Matthew had raised an eyebrow and said matter-of-factly: "I'm not at all in sympathy. He's keeping alive the wrong kind of people. The money is misspent. It would be better used to help poor white people."

Perhaps to confirm his views about "undependable French niggers," Matthew traveled to Deschapelles to see how his brother was doing. He stayed only three days. "Dreadful place—Haiti," he said cheerfully. "And that Larry—he's chasing a dream."

But a few months after his visit, Matthew transferred fifteen thousand dollars to the Grant Foundation so that the dreamer could keep on dreaming. Better than anyone, he knew that stories of Larry Mellon's reserve wealth were fable, because most of his family inheritance was tied up in trust funds for the children. Without outside contributions, the hospital would go broke.

Yet in spite of their valiant efforts, few of the whites involved in Deschapelles made much impact on the Haitians. The peasants believed that all white men could get plenty of money without working too hard for it. So why should they hesitate to give most of their time and money to poor people?

At home during the day, wives of doctors were pestered by beggars. And village children kept pestering visiting *blancs* with their only English sentence: "Give me five cents."

Gwen Mellon once presented a little house to a homeless old couple. They came to her a day later, smiling. "Now we're your responsibility," they said. "You must give us food, too."

Mellon himself was the easiest prey. Every time he was about to refuse a beggar, he would mutter: "Well, maybe I'd do the same thing if I were in this fellow's boots." And then he would hand over a gourde.

Many patients arriving at the hospital's front desk told Gwen sorrowfully that they had no money. She would remonstrate in rapid Creole and, as often as not, tattered gourde notes would be produced from a deep pocket or from a tiny paper pouch tied around the sick person's neck.

Yet nobody could say that the peasants envied the white people their money or their way of life. These Haitians had neither an inferiority complex nor a chip on their shoulders. Much as they respected the white man's medicine, they felt *blancs* had made life unnecessarily complicated and burdensome for themselves. All a man really needed for happiness was a *caille,* a garden, a shirt, a pair of pants, plenty of food, and two or three women. *Blancs* had endless possessions and endless problems.

Peasants could be seen searching the faces of the serious-looking doctors and wan nurses for signs of life, zest, and devilry. Sometimes, of course, they found it. Many other times they shrugged and turned away. White people had acquired cleverness and riches at the expense of sensuality and *joie de vivre.* Whenever peasants were not curbed by the white man's gravity, they were on fire with life. They really did not give a damn about anything except enjoying each other's company during their short stay on earth.

Their strange mixture of gaiety and suffering was not apparent at the hospital, but it could be found and felt by any doctor who ventured beyond the white encampment at Deschapelles—even among peasants on their way to the hospital for treatment on clinic mornings.

A young physician once rode the 7 A.M. "bus" from Saint Marc to Deschapelles. This was a brightly painted, ancient truck with plank seats running lengthwise along each side of the canopied back. The peasants called the truck a *tap-tap;* they entered it with as great dignity as if they were boarding a Rolls-Royce limousine.

The doctor squirmed self-consciously in his seat for the first few miles in the *tap-tap* and gazed stonily at the countryside. But nobody was at all interested in him. The sick people in the truck were enjoying themselves thoroughly; he could either join them or stay aloof as he wished.

On the seat opposite, a mother was trying to quiet her crying baby. A peasant boy leaned over and gave the little girl a sip from a tilted bottle of water, and, her thirst quenched, the child went to sleep. Then the *tap-tap* stopped while a mother helped her teen-age son climb into the back. He wept with pain and he had a towel wrapped around his head as sick people often did. A less ailing man offered the boy his seat, then scrambled outside to ride the rest of the way on the roof.

This happened all along the route. Men immediately vacated seats to make room for a woman or a man sicker than themselves. When the roof was filled, men knelt in the narrow middle aisle, and when the aisle was jammed, they hung on to the back of the bus.

Clutched in their hands were white slips of paper with HÔPITAL ALBERT SCHWEITZER printed on top. They were the only tickets for this *tap-tap* ride.

Two handsome young peasant women had a spirited conversation at one end of the truck, sharing gossip in loud, chuckling voices for the enjoyment of all the other passengers. They paused briefly to commiserate with a mother cradling a blind baby, then started chattering again. Their faces kept changing expression and they often broke into rippling laughter. When the *tap-tap* went over a bump, causing a bone-shaking jolt in the back, their laughter became a gleeful shout.

By the time the bus neared Deschapelles, only a few of the men were left seated. Yet one of these jumped off and held a baby while a mother clambered aboard. Returning the baby, he took the last place on the rear step. At least thirty, ragged, ailing people jammed that little truck, yet they probably were the best mannered bus-load on earth at that moment.

Except for the very sick and aged, the only man still sitting inside at this stage of the trip was the *blanc*. He had not known in advance of courtly Haitian manners, nor how many places other than a seat a man could occupy on a bus.

During the long journey, there had been no familiar, "Eh, *blanc,* give me a cigarette." "Eh, *blanc,* give me five cents." The doctor, in the midst of the peasantry, was sharing a fragment of their lives on their terms.

As the *tap-tap* halted outside the hospital, the two gossipers must have said something really funny, for the whole crowd guffawed. The doctor, catching no more than a word or two, missed the joke. He grinned weakly.

"Eh, *blanc,*" said a feeble old man, tapping him on the knee, "you should learn our language."

This was the side of the Haitian peasant that Mellon understood so well. He was anguished because empty supper bowls and creeping disease were sapping the vitality of these dancing people.

His real job was not to change this society he liked and admired, but to fill the bowls and kill the diseases so the peasants could give full vent to life again.

POVERTY AND IGNORANCE were the real scourges of the Artibonite Valley. If both were remedied, disease would be reduced and the peasants could eat regularly. They could also pay their bills at the Hôpital Albert Schweitzer, thus ensuring its survival and expansion. Once ignorance was overcome the people would be able to understand Mellon's medicine and the importance of hygiene and sickness prevention.

The way the doctor saw it, the peasants needed a community development program as much as, if not more than, medicine.

The teaching of crafts and the establishment of workshops seemed to Mellon the surest way to start. He was advised differently, however, by four educationalists from Michigan State sent down by Emory Ross, Schweitzer's man in New York, to help devise a program. Ross was now a director of Mellon's hospital. Education must be the keynote, the Michigan State professors said. This would have a chain reaction leading the peasants to a variety of enterprises. Mellon's faith in their idea was confirmed by a meeting in New York with a man named James Yen. A Yale-educated Chinese, Yen had contrived a simplified Chinese alphabet during World War I service with the YMCA in France and had taught thousands of illiterate coolies working on defense roads there how to read and write. In time, twenty million Chinese became literate through the Yen method.

It would take a small miracle to match Yen's accomplishment in the Artibonite Valley, but Mellon went ahead. He had ceased counting the odds against success.

Emory Ross provided the small miracle by sending to Deschapelles the brilliant missionary team of the Reverend Lloyd Shirer and his wife Margaret. The Shirers, just back from Africa, had gone to see Ross in New York to discuss which of five assignments they should choose next. Ross gave them a sixth alternative, that of heading the community development at Mellon's hospital. They flew down to Haiti immediately.

Shirer, a churchman with connections, solved the first problem by getting USAID to produce all the necessary textbooks. Then lessons in the reading and writing of Creole commenced at Deschapelles. Since the theme of community development was "to aid the people to live healthier, happier lives and to raise their own standard of living by self-help," Mellon did not make it entirely free. Peasant students had to pay a gourde and a half for a literacy kit of three textbooks, a copy book, and a pencil.

The response was incredible. Hundreds of peasants applied for lessons, and they learned quickly. After three months of study they were no longer classed as illiterates. Reluctant ones were coaxed along by being taught how to write their names. Amazed at how easily they could learn this, and proud of the prestige it gave them, they stayed on for the full course.

Top scholars from the hospital classes were appointed as monitors and sent out to spread learning through the valley and hills. Graduates were rewarded with a literacy certificate signed by Mellon as well as a free copy of the New Testament in Creole. This inducement brought steady enrollments; students soon numbered in the thousands. There came a time when nearly a hundred monitors were in action, each teaching a class of twenty or thirty peasants. Monsieur Delinois alone sponsored twenty classes in one section of the mountains.

The course was not too exacting because the Creole language was presented in the books as it was spoken—simple, phonetic, and uncomplicated by formal grammar. The French word for cloth, *toile,* was pronounced "twal" in Creole. And that was how it was written. A *chapeau* was "chapo" and *histoire* was "istwa."

Once a student had mastered Creole, he could also learn French or English from members of the Deschapelles medical staff. They gave lessons several nights each week at the newly constructed community center wing. Although there were not as many in these classes, a number of peasants were often to be seen engrossed in English primers at the noon work break.

Encouraged by the successes in literacy, Mellon and the Shirers made a concerted attempt at health education. But no reward of prestige could be offered here. It proved to be a dogged, disappointing struggle.

Instead of drinking water from polluted streams and canals, the peasants were advised by Mellon to tap springs in the hills and pipe clean water down to fountains in the market places. The people were not impressed with the idea.

So Mellon, knowing that he would have to show them the benefits, bought thousands of feet of narrow pipe and trudged off himself to find a lively spring. Helped by curious volunteers, he put a valve on the spring and dug a ditch for the pipe right to the market at Verrettes. At each joint in the pipeline he made the Haitians go back and cover the exposed portion. For once the line was down and the fountain flowing, the peasants would see no sense in chasing up the hill to bury the pipe.

Villagers were delighted when the clear spring water gushed at Verrettes, and they were more eager to help when pipelines were laid to other places. Some of them actually paid part of the cost. Roughly two thousand dollars were needed to install and feed each fountain with water. Peasant contributions amounted to about two hundred dollars a fountain. They felt they were not getting something for nothing and Mellon himself was pleased.

The community development team explained why the fountains were so important: bad water could cause typhoid and dysentery. But again Mellon's men ran up against a mental block about disease prevention. If a peasant lost control of his bowels, he usually thought that someone had put a voodoo hex on him. For a *blanc* to blame the impure water seemed pretty simple-minded. And in a stream a mile from the Verrettes fountain, women could still be seen washing, drinking, and urinating in already polluted water.

Mellon and his field workers labored themselves on many of the home health safety measures. Out of sheer politeness, peasants accepted their sweat and suggestions. Gradually, however, community leaders were persuaded to set an example by building lips on their household wells so that mud and muck would not be washed into the water every time it rained. They were shown how to raise their cooking fires on little platforms above the ground, thus preventing children from falling into the fires and stopping the hungry dogs from slobbering over the cooking pots. Latrines were built for the peasants, *cailles* were equipped with stoves and chimneys, and broken-down huts were replaced with more solid dwellings of clay and cement structure.

Still the advances in public health were, at best, faltering. Mellon's community development budget of thirty thousand dollars a year was totally inadequate for an effective program, even for his small slice of Haiti. And as for the prevention of communicable diseases, there he was doomed to failure; this had to be a nation-wide project.

Years before, a successful onslaught against yaws had been carried on right through the country. UNESCO had done the same thing against malaria, although this disease could hardly be eradicated. That, however, was the extent of public health in Haiti. Tuberculosis and venereal disease, both widespread and both preventable, were neglected. No broad-scale attempt was made to correct unsanitary living conditions and most peasants had worms.

At Deschapelles one day a peasant woman vomited a worm, causing a Haitian doctor to fire up with anger.

"Is that what I'm going to be all my life," he snapped, "a worm doctor? We're on a treadmill here. Day after day, the same sicknesses, and most of them need not be, if we could only educate, immunize, vaccinate."

Mellon had no reply for outbursts like this. The most he could do was to scratch the surface and pray he was leaving a mark. Besides the immunization of babies at the hospital, a team was sent out every week to inoculate school children. For every child treated, however, there were a hundred who could not be reached.

In contrast to this bleak outlook, however, community development was making fine headway in other areas. Recreation was an important part of the plan for better living. A choir was organized at the hospital, and, with Charlie Ponte's help, three brass bands were equipped and trained. Football games and concerts were sponsored as a relief from the blood and scuffle of the Saturday afternoon cockfights staged by the peasant bucks just down the road from Deschapelles. As with voodoo, the Mellons did not interfere with this native form of entertainment. Opportunities for having a good time in the valley were all too infrequent.

Classes in carpentry and ceramics were started to give dozens of teen-age boys a trade, or, in Gandhi's words, "a cottage industry." The care and originality the lads showed in tackling assignments satisfied Mellon that the strong grain of individualism and the nudging ambition within the community were well worth nourishing. This was to be part of the healing process for this section of Haiti, a spreading of the hospital influence into many spheres.

Sewing centers became important in the program, for here Mellon was able to offer the women what they needed most desperately—a job with good wages.

A main sewing room was installed in the community center wing and others were set up in the villages. Sewing machines and material were supplied. Girls were hired, trained, and then paid a few dollars a week for their labor. Uniforms, pajamas, smocks, and clothes were made for poor patients.

A pretty young Haitian named Sultane showed what a

peasant girl could do with a regular income. In two years of working as a seamstress at twenty-five dollars a month, Sultane saved two hundred and fifty dollars.

This was more than most valley people put aside in a lifetime, enough indeed to buy an acre of good land and a home. Sultane, however, was biding her time. The father of her illegitimate daughter could not get his family's blessing to marry her. Sultane complained that her lover was under his mother's thumb. But since she was now a girl of independent means she had no need to grovel to anyone. She and her daughter had their own four-roomed *caille* in Sultane's family compound. Her bedroom was the envy of the neighborhood; it contained a fine bed of polished wood, a hanging closet filled with dresses, and a low, mirrored dressing table strewn with earrings, gold brush-and-comb set, glass-framed pictures, and her silver wrist watch.

Mellon had worried that an aunt or uncle might "borrow" from Sultane's hoard of dollars. But being a true career girl, she had salted away the money in the hospital's Mutual Credit Society. Whenever she was asked for money, she said it was locked up at Deschapelles and could not be touched for a long, long time.

The best sewing center proved to be the one at Estrale, a village tucked away in the dry millet fields some miles from the hospital.

Estrale was a woebegone place when Mellon first encountered it. The huts were crumbling to dust, the land around was parched, and nobody seemed to be about but a horde of miserable naked children. The few listless, sad-eyed adults whom Mellon rounded up agreed that Estrale was starving to death. They could only hope that God would intervene and set things right again.

Mellon considered it a disaster area. He set up a day nursery with a good midday meal of CARE food for the children, while the adults went out to seek work. Not wanting to offer complete charity, he made a nominal charge of ten cents a week for each child. Nobody, however, paid. Then, seeking a different way to help the village get back on its feet, Mellon rented an old building and launched a sewing center. The women of Estrale warmed to this immediately; they were willing to do anything to earn a steady income.

Within months, the village had taken on new vigor. Huts were repaired and the doors were painted with blues and pinks. Clothes appeared on the children and sandals on the women. And the last hint of stagnancy disappeared when Mellon tapped his main water pipe and brought in a branch line to the center of the village.

The valley contained many places like Estrale, villages where death was at the door and trying to force its way in. Mellon knew time and money would be needed, but he vowed to hold the door against death and snap these towns out of their coma, one by one.

Time was Mellon's shortest commodity. For four years he had worked as a physician on full hospital call; now he had added the roles of literacy teacher, pipe-layer, latrine-builder and sewing center superintendent. The burden was too much. Gwen worried because he often came home for lunch white and shaking after hours of hard physical labor in the valley.

When the Shirers prepared to leave Haiti to resume their African work, Mellon decided to give up his doctoring and concentrate on community development. The hospital was well staffed and running smoothly now. Ward capacity was being stretched to take one hundred and fifty patients at a pinch.

For the outside work, Mellon received help from young men sent to Haiti by the Mennonite Central Committee. The United States Government permitted them to spend two years of community service in a foreign land instead of doing the usual military stint. With the Mennonite nurses already at the hospital, Deschapelles now had a sizable group of this sect. They made a conscientious, if somber, team.

Soon after this, an orphan peasant girl of sixteen was crippled in a truck accident. The neighbors with whom she had been living refused to take her back from the hospital because she could no longer work for them.

"Will you accept her if she pays for her room and food?" Mellon asked them. Having experienced similar callousness before, he did not waste time on a lecture.

The neighbors agreed that they would, though they wondered how a paraplegic girl could earn money. Mellon, however, had a brilliant solution to the problem. Buying a basket of raw cotton from a peasant, he hired the handicapped girl to sit at home, pick out the seeds, and roll the soft cotton into one-inch balls. These wads were later sterilized and used at the hospital. Since there was a continuing demand for these cotton balls, the girl soon had a permanent job which paid a few dollars a month. She became one of the most popular boarders in the valley, and out of this grew the most successful of all the cottage industries, the cotton project.

Cotton grew wild in the Haitian hills and Mellon bought liberally from the harvest. He established a cotton project among out-of-work families, paying some to pick out the seeds, and others to wind the clean tufts into spools of thick cotton thread. The carpentry boys built hand looms and weaving shops were established here and there just as sewing centers had been earlier.

Soon, throughout the district, peasants could be seen hunched over their baskets of cotton, picking and winding. One enthusiastic cotton picker was a woman with five children, whose soldier husband had deserted her after he had been accidentally shot in the head. The wound healed, but the man complained that his family gave him a headache so he moved out. Others involved in the cotton project had similar stories of hardship. To them, this new source of income meant the difference between eating and going hungry. It was no sinecure, however, because the piecework rate gave only a dollar a week to many. Paying for the spools on a weight basis, Mellon was a familiar—and welcome—sight as he tramped about the valley with an old set of vegetable scales in his hand.

The program was expected to pay for itself, and the rate was set according to the market value of the finished products. The looms turned out rugs, drapes, and upholstery material worth three dollars a yard before being shipped from Deschapelles, and Mellon estimated his costs from that figure. Gwen Mellon used much of the material to furnish hospital rooms and the doctors' apartments and houses. The surplus was shipped to the United States for sale, one of the few uniquely Haitian products available. The only imported gadget employed in the project was the metal comb used at first to gather the cotton on the looms. Determined to make the whole industry self-sufficient, Mellon later adopted a locally made bamboo comb.

In time, the project expanded to provide full support for one hundred Haitian families. A weakness was the limited variety of woven goods, but Mellon remedied this by flying to Guatemala and bringing back Luis Garcia, the best Guatemalan weaver he could find.

Even at this stage Mellon was still feeling his way in community development, and when he hit on an idea that worked as well as the cotton project, he sought expert advice to perfect it.

Animal husbandry was another field he wanted to develop and so he brought to Haiti a brilliant young Cornell veterinarian graduate. Julian Strauss showed peasants how to keep their animals healthy and how to make the pigs and chickens fatter for the slaughter.

"If you want to know the basic condition of any country," a Haitian once said, "just look at the animals." In Haiti, the farm stock ranked among the mangiest critters in the Americas.

In the animal program, Mellon's dual purpose was to increase peasant income and to give a happier life to the animals, no matter how short that span might be. He himself was too much the Schweitzer disciple to step on a bug or kill a green snake living in a tree near his house. Peachy, his dog, was a little mutt he had discovered some years before, whimpering and homeless on the steps at Tulane.

According to a feeble joke told at Deschapelles, Mellon was driving to Port-au-Prince one day all dressed up in his best suit. He came upon a man and his horse knocked down on the road by a truck. Seeing the horse in agony with a broken leg, Mellon stripped off his suit, grabbed a knife, and administered the merciful death thrust. This grisly story brought shouts of laughter from Haitians. They had so little feeling for suffering animals that Mellon's action seemed to them the height of *blanc* idiosyncrasy.

Miss Pete, however, related a true story about the time Mellon stopped his car by a group of peasant women beating a mule half to death in an attempt to get it to move. The mule stood its ground, head slumped and legs rooted. With never a word, Mellon walked behind the animal and gave its tail a tweak. The mule ambled off, leaving the women dumbstruck, their sticks halted in mid-air.

There is a right way and a wrong way to deal with animals. Mellon "gentled" them. He had done this when breaking in wild horses on his Arizona ranch, and he did it now in Haiti with equal success.

Julian Strauss extended the practice to pigs. Pamper a pig, said Strauss, and he would return the favor doubly in pork. With this in mind, he began a long and stubborn campaign to get the peasants to build pig "parlors" with cement floors and thatched roofs. Some complied, and thus community development notched another small victory over poverty.

HOW CAN I FOLLOW in your footsteps and do some work like yours in a needy country?"

Now that his mission was better known abroad, Mellon was receiving dozens of letters from men who asked this question in one form or another. Remembering his own first letters to Schweitzer and the encouraging response from the old man, Mellon always replied to such inquiries. Yet because he had little gift for words, he found it difficult to describe the difference between the theory and practice of humanitarianism. The work, he felt, must be seen at first-hand, and experienced, to be understood.

His favorite anecdote concerned a man who went to Lambaréné to talk over the finer points of Schweitzer's philosophy of reverence for life.

"Before the theory, a little example," Schweitzer had said. He had put the man to work, helping him build a bridge across a stream for the natives. While they were lugging heavy timbers about in the broiling sun at the end of the fifth day, Schweitzer paused to remind his sweating visitor that they had not yet got around to philosophy.

"It's hardly necessary now," said the visitor, blowing on his blistered hands. "I see—and feel—what you mean."

Whenever Mellon's correspondents suggested a personal visit to Deschapelles, he invited them to come ahead. But the Haitian interior seemed a strange and lonely place to newcomers and they rarely stayed long enough to really understand the work being done in the valley.

"Perhaps, for example, an insurance agent from Omaha who thinks he wants to change his life and do this kind of thing will fly down," Mellon says wryly. "I pick him up at the airport at Port-au-Prince, bring him out to the valley and show him around. A few days later, having learned nothing, he decides to whizz off. I drive him back to the airport, and that's that. I never hear from him again."

One visitor, an Australian named Michelmore, the author of this book, first met Mellon on just such a tour. At the time, Julian Strauss was on the job and community development was still inching ahead on a trial-and-error basis.

I found then that Mellon gave no "guided" tours. You were expected to tag along while he went about his chores, listen while he thought out loud, and draw your own conclusions about the man and his work. He never tried to convert anyone to his way of life.

"Look," the doctor told me some time later, "it's like getting married. The only way to test whether you're going to like it is to try it. You don't have to stay stuck in the wilds if you find you don't like it. But if you do like it, you won't feel enslaved. A man who is very fond of his wife does not feel tied down."

Early one morning I tracked Mellon's white Chevrolet to a field near the hospital. A peasant directed me further to a low building of concrete block and chicken wire. I walked inside and called Mellon's name. A white man bent over a large barrel lifted his head and said, "I'm Dr. Mellon."

He looked lean, tallish, though slightly stooped. There was a handkerchief tied around his nose and mouth. His shirt was wet with perspiration and clinging to his chest. The temperature inside that block house must have been ninety-five degrees. Inside the barrel, it was probably a hundred and ten.

I introduced myself and Mellon said I was welcome to look around. Still keeping the handkerchief on his face, he gestured around the building and said, "What we're doing here is finding a way for the people to pay their hospital bills."

Then, removing his mask, he said something in Creole to two peasants watching him at the barrel. Apparently they were cotton pickers. Mellon told me that raw cotton in the barrel had been handpicked clean of seed. It was better done by hand because a machine broke the staple too short. The seed had been kept in a four-gallon drum for pig feed.

"We pay them two dollars for every five pounds of cotton they pick clean," he said, reaching into his pocket and counting out some gourde notes for the two Haitians. Mellon's wallet, I soon discovered, was a beautiful sight to Haitian peasants.

The American doctor now moved across the room to talk with some girls working at hand looms, then we walked to another building where about fifteen teen-agers were making tables and chairs.

"Must have a word with these boys," said Mellon. "The man who taught the carpentry class was killed in a road accident on his way to Port-au-Prince yesterday. His loss has thrown us into a tailspin."

For ten minutes he spoke quietly to the boys, eulogizing their late instructor and suggesting that he would have wanted them to go on working with their projects until another teacher could be found.

Mellon seemed thoughtful as we climbed into his car. I chose that moment to ask the kind of sweeping, eager-beaver questions that he deplores. They appear idiotic now: Did he condemn the arms race? Was he in favor of moral rearmament? Was he trying to put just one part of the troubled world in order?

After pointing out politely that he personally could not influence East-West relations, Mellon said the notion expressed in the last question was too all-comprehensive. "You throw a stone and who knows how far it will go," he said. "We aren't wise enough to tell. But if our work here indirectly causes improvement in some valley in Peru, for instance, we'll feel that we're doing some good."

A few miles down the road two peasants flagged the car to a halt. The younger man wanted to hitch a ride. He claimed to be the cousin of the third Haitian president before the last one, and Mellon so introduced him to me. The other man, senile and demented, hung on the door and asked for *cob*—money. Haiti has so many beggars that a visitor usually hardens and refuses every one. And in this country where cars are scarce, people clamor for rides whether they need to go anywhere or not. Despite his many years in the valley, Mellon showed no irritation at the familiar requests. The former president's cousin got his ride and the old man was given a gourde.

Out on a back road we left Mellon's car and boarded a station wagon driven by Julian Strauss. The young vet complained that he was damn tired of peasants using his wagon as a taxi. He wanted permission to put a *no passengers* sign on his front window. Mellon agreed readily.

Strauss, who had a bold air about him, bounced his wagon off into the bush, keeping approximately to two deep wheel tracks. Eventually we parked and Strauss led the way up a rocky path through thin corn stalks. Mellon, following behind, asked the lean, handsome vet if it would be all right to give young pigs to peasants without previous experience in raising the creatures.

"No," said Strauss, "the best thing is to give pigs to people who have shown they know how to handle them. It is not wise even to give them to Haitians with lousy pigs because they'll soon make the new pigs just as lousy. I know that sounds tough, but it's only common sense."

Mellon turned to me. "We're not always sure what is the best thing to do. We can only try and hope to do what's right."

"It may seem strange to worry about details like this," Strauss cut in, "but I remember reading about a valley in Chile. Some experts introduced a new corn there. It matured faster, was fatter in the cob, tasted better, was superior in every way. The peasants were very enthusiastic; they planted it over the entire valley. It so happened that the peasants used a lot of the dried corn seeds for grinding into flour, and this new corn proved to be a little too hard. It was no good for homemade flour, but they discovered that it made an excellent liquor. Now they're a valley of alcoholics."

At this point we came to a collection of four thatched huts.

Eight or nine youngsters, most of them naked, were playing about in the dust. Mellon shook hands with the oldest, a boy around fourteen, who was wearing a surprisingly good pair of pants rolled to the knee. The parents were away so we moved further up the trail to a second group of huts. There was another clutter of naked children, but this time several peasant men and women as well. Mellon and Strauss shook hands all around and explained who they were.

"Ah, yes," said an old crone, "from Madame Mellon's hospital."

The doctor let the comment pass and bent forward to pat the bloated stomach of a little girl with malnutrition. I saw tears glisten in his eyes. "Didn't you get milk for her from the hospital?" he asked the mother, a pregnant woman with the drowsiness often caused by malaria. The Haitian told the doctor she had received dried milk but had not yet learned how to mix it. Mellon asked for the package, then gave her careful instructions.

As we walked over to inspect the family pig tethered to a nearby tree and wallowing listlessly in mud, I saw his eyes glisten. "We must keep at it," he said. "Another child living around here was cured of malnutrition because we persuaded the mother to feed it cow's milk. The family owned a cow but weren't using the milk. Now the cow's gone dry, the child is slipping back, and the parents say they can't afford another cow."

Meanwhile Strauss was trying to convince one of the men that if he built a cheap shelter for the family pig and put down a cement floor, it would become twice as fat in half the time. The American insisted that the man's pig was so painfully thin because of worms. These parasites had infected the hog as it lay unprotected on the bare ground.

"A man in town put his pigs in a hut with a floor and got twenty-three dollars each for them at the market," Strauss told the peasant. "And they weren't a year old."

The peasant realized that he would be lucky to get ten dollars for his mangy pig, already a full three years old. Although he listened attentively, he did not show any real interest until Strauss offered to trade cement for lime. As the vet talked, we were standing on a hill of limestone.

This trade proposition was a last resort. On the pig project Strauss liked the peasants to buy the cement. For a pig hut floor a man needed three sacks of cement and, at a dollar a sack, he had enough invested to want to do a good job. The budget for the animal side of the community development scheme was a mere fifteen hundred dollars a year. Strauss felt that success could be measured in how little he had to spend on losing trades like this cement-for-lime deal.

Mellon, however, was reasonably pleased with the reaction, saying, "If we get one or two peasants interested in these pig houses in each area, then the practice will spread quickly."

Driving back down the bush track, we were stopped outside the village of Liancourt by a Haitian who wanted Mellon and Strauss to see his pigs. They were snorting and scuffling about on a sloping cement platform fenced with rough-cut branches and roofed with straw. The hogs looked sleek and clean, even frisky. Mellon gave a tug on a corner post to show the peasant he admired its sturdy construction. "Magnifique," he said. The man beamed at the compliment.

In Liancourt we came across one of Strauss's native assistants vaccinating chickens against Newcastle's disease, a fatal sickness once the ruin of valley flocks.

The chicken vaccination campaign had been an accidental success. Peasants were skeptical at first, and the drive was not helped when a villager of some prestige refused to use the needle on a prize fighting cock worth twenty dollars. A week later, however, the cock died from Newcastle's disease. When his owner bought a replacement, he decided to risk the vaccination. The second cock lived on to win fight after fight. The owner was delighted and trumpeted the magic of Strauss's vaccine up and down the valley. Peasants were soon clamoring to have their poultry treated.

"We charge three cents a shot and actually make a profit," Strauss said happily. "Of course, when they can't pay right away, we extend credit." He pointed to a stack of IOU's clipped on the sunshield inside his station wagon. Apparently Strauss intended to collect every penny.

Mellon gave him a quick look of approval. He liked the vet's bluff approach. But then I remembered how easily the crazy old man had begged a gourde from him, the tears in his eyes when he rubbed the stomach of the child with malnutrition, how pleased he had been when the old crone gave him a plump green shaddock. Mellon had been hefting it in his hand ever since. I was sure he would wash the dirt and dung from the fruit when he got home and have it for lunch. If these two white men were equally tough and equally tender, Mellon's hard core must be hidden deep inside.

That afternoon I went out again with Strauss, this time accompanied by a Swiss nurse who wanted to see more of the valley. Our errand was to deliver four bags of cement to a peasant in the eastern hills beyond the village of Desarmes. It was a good opportunity to study Strauss, who was obviously the type of man Mellon liked on his team.

"My wife Katie and I love it down here," the vet said as we headed up the road. "We find life more satisfying than in the States. And we enjoy being with the Mellons. To my mind, Dr. Mellon is still the cowboy, riding the range and practicing his homespun philosophy . . . Yippee!"

Cresting a hill we had just descended into a ravine. A creek cut across the road and several nude bathing beauties scuttled for cover at the sight of us. One statuesque girl, loping up the stream, gave a sultry look over her shoulder at Strauss's yell.

"I usually like to sneak up on them," the vet said with an exaggerated leer. After the somber piety of some of the hospital staff, Strauss was a refreshing character. I could see why people said he "goes over well with the peasants."

Five miles off the main track, while we were passing a group of huts perched on a hillside, a man came running to intercept the wagon. "Doctor! Doctor!" he cried in Creole. "Girl sick. Girl sick." And he rubbed his stomach vigorously to show what he meant.

Strauss jammed on the brakes and strode off for the huts with his vet bag. It contained a sterilizer, cotton, tranquillizers, and a hypodermic needle—all designed for treating dairy cows.

Inside a tiny, two-roomed, dirt-floored *caille,* Strauss and the Swiss nurse found a girl around eighteen kneeling on a straw mat. There was a blood-soaked blanket between her legs. At the entrance of the *blancs,* she started up a pitiful wailing.

One of the family explained that the girl had been hemorrhaging for twelve hours, apparently suffering a miscarriage in her fifth month of pregnancy. The nurse cleaned her and made a pack from sterilized cotton in Strauss's bag. Then the patient was made to lie back with her feet up.

The hemorrhage continued, however, so after he had delivered the cement, Strauss padded the back of his wagon with straw mats to give the girl as restful a drive as possible to the hospital. Even so, the wagon clattered over rocks and splashed through mud, causing the patient to wail louder and louder.

Strauss winced every time she hit a high note. "Poor girl," he said, "she probably thinks she's going straight to Hell."

He kept on talking to take his mind off the patient in the back. "Down here you harden yourself to sickness and suffering. It's like a battlefield really. I had my baptism back in Utica. One summer I worked as an ambulance driver and once we were called out on an accident where a car had hit a bridge. A husband and wife had been inside. The man was dead, his head virtually severed. The woman was seriously injured and shocked, but all the way to the hospital she kept singing hymns and trying to hold her husband's head back in place. You see, you have to become immune to tragedy like this."

When we reached the hospital, Strauss called the orderlies. The girl was quickly loaded onto a stretcher and taken to a ward. The strangeness of the place upset her even more. Her cries echoed along the corridors and stopped Strauss as he was pushing through the front door to go home. "Ah, well," he said, turning on his heel, "maybe I better go talk to her."

Mellon had complained that most visitors did not learn

anything about his mission of mercy, but I felt that this afternoon had given me a vivid insight into both the urgency and humaneness of the work he had founded. Mellon himself could not have had a more dramatic afternoon.

A nurse said he was home resting after spending some time in the hospital helping tend a gravely ill baby. The infant had needed a transfusion of O-negative blood which was rare.

"Fortunately," said the nurse, "Dr. Mellon is O-negative, so he gave the baby another pint of his blood."

I asked what she meant by "another."

"He gave a pint yesterday, too," she said. "And it's been only a few weeks since his last donation. I don't know how he stands up!"

While much of Deschapelles seemed to be a routine of clinic days and weighing cotton and persuading peasants to build pig parlors, life there was never lived in a straight line. It was always uphill, with death lapping at the climbing feet, and Mellon and his men stationed along the way to help the peasants over the worst patches. There was unrelenting pressure in this work of succor, and hard physical labor. Often the doctors were pushed to the limits of endurance, almost brought to their knees and left panting.

On a memorable Saturday during my first visit, Harold May had opened up a man to remedy what he thought was a swelling of the aorta. The man's agony and other symptoms suggested that it had to be something of the kind. The aorta, however, proved to be normal, so May closed him up. Perhaps the patient had a stomach abscess. The necessary incision was made, but no abscess was found either. May then stood over his patient, uncertain what to do next. The nurses waited quietly for instructions. May felt very alone. The peasant's life depended on what he did in the next few hours. And May could not even take a walk to clear his head, or succumb to normal mortal nervousness.

He cut the man open again now, from chest to loin and right across the belly. Searching desperately for the mysterious ailment, he found it at last—aneurysm, a dilation of the veins. Meticulously during hours of tedious surgery, he cut away at the mass of excess fiber swelling the man's insides. When the patient was clean, May sewed him up and held the door while nurses wheeled him back to the ward.

Then the surgeon's knees started to buckle. He looked at his watch. It was 1 A.M. Dr. May had been on his feet, operating on one man, for thirteen hours.

I complimented him on his feat the following day, but he merely said, "I'm a surgeon, so it's my job to operate on sick people."

Mellon reacted in the same way when I spoke to him about his giving blood.

Valor had become commonplace at Deschapelles because that quality was required all the time. Life—or rather, how a man could use his vitality—was notched to a higher level. It brought to mind Schweitzer's notions about "adventures for the soul," and how they brought out strength and daring in a man.

Indeed, the mark of Schweitzer could be seen everywhere at Mellon's hospital. Healthy, talented men were spending a good measure of their own blessings on others less fortunate. Gandhi, of course, had influenced the community development program, but it also echoed Schweitzer's philosophy of personal action in the cause of brotherhood. Never mind the skepticism of the people in need, Schweitzer had said, and never mind the rebuff. Mellon, too, had encountered both barriers and had not been deterred.

Over the centuries, many thinkers have wondered how to make humanitarianism sound more dramatic and spectacular so that more people will take up such a career. Actually this is impossible because—again according to Dr. Schweitzer—there is no reward for the work except the privilege of doing it.

Would a man really rejoice in occupying himself exclusively with the needs of others? The only way to find out, Mellon believed, was to try and see. He was doing exactly this now and his life had become the promised adventure of the soul.

10

THE MORE Mellon pushed on with his community development, the more other foreigners in Haiti speculated that he was planning his own downfall. According to these "experts," the Negro chieftains in Port-au-Prince did not want the peasants educated and made more self-sufficient. The politicians' unchallenged power depended on the ignorance and poverty of the peasants.

If Mellon heard this speculation, he ignored it. Nor would he say a word against the conduct of the ruling clique, although they were becoming so ruthless that some American doctors bound for work at Deschapelles checked first with the State Department to see if Haiti was safe for a white man.

Through a series of political crises and bloody witch-hunts, murder and extortion, Mellon's attitude did not waver. He considered himself a guest in Haiti and he had a job to do locally in the Artibonite Valley. It was none of his business how the country was managed. And it was up to him to obey the rules of the management whatever they were.

When one of the doctors complained that peasants walked in the middle of the road and got in the way of cars, Mellon sharply reminded him, "It's their road, you know."

Events did show, however, that he would not be getting much help in rescuing the peasants, because Haiti would continue to be an urchin on the doorstep of the Americas. The black bureaucracy in Port-au-Prince would still rule with fear and siphon off what money it could from the thinning budget and foreign aid for personal pleasures and for security against the day when it would be chased from Haiti. Foreign newsmen visiting Haiti heard stories of terror and graft in Port-au-Prince, and then skedaddled to write articles, as novelist Graham Greene did, about "the nightmare republic." The articles adversely affected Haitian trade, frightened away tourists, and made the Port-au-Prince rulers even greedier and fiercer. They allowed the irrigation project in the Artibonite to falter and did not worry when Chuck Wiggin, the driving force, was posted to another country. The big losers, of course, were the four million peasants. Their horizons were never pushed back.

Magloire had been hounded out of the country, and, after seven makeshift governments, Duvalier was installed as president. His background as a liberal, kindly physician did not count now. The men who put him in office demanded strength and cunning. Otherwise he would have to go. Duvalier, a weak sort, decided to play the game. As an enticement to Washington to refresh the Haitian budget, he cranked the ODVA into action again, starting a few projects like a model peasant village north of the capital.

Any clear-thinking official of the U.S. State Department could have gone to Haiti, looked around for a few days, and told Duvalier of an honest way in which to treble his budget. The tourist potential of the place was obvious. Other resort islands in the Caribbean, like Puerto Rico and Jamaica, were tired and sexless by comparison. Haiti had the best rum in the world, some of the most beautiful women, excellent Creole cooking, a superb winter climate, breathtaking scenery, a unique culture, and a hint of dark mystery in the air. American foreign aid could have been granted specifically for tourist promotion. Instead, millions of dollars were shoveled into the open maw of bureaucracy. Graft was easily covered up with phony requisition forms, many of which Duvalier did not even see.

One USAID man in Haiti later estimated that eleven out of twenty-four million dollars sent from Washington was stolen by the grafters. "It's a country of thieves," his wife added. "I lock my doors and check the windows every night, and even then I'm scared to go to bed."

This couple, like many others attached to USAID in Haiti, lived in a jaded American colony in Pétionville. They rarely visited the country areas, made no attempt to learn the language and mixed with the Haitians as little as possible. In their cocktail hour conversation, they were prone to voice approval of the British colonial system, although they agreed that the Administration in Washington was too socialistic to see things their way.

Haitian Government officials felt they were swindling these empty-headed *blancs* rather than some impersonal money machine called USAID.

Because he was the number one witch doctor and was expected to be able to strike a man dead with a lifted finger, Duvalier recruited a tough group of henchmen to seek out opponents saying even one word against him. He called his secret police group the National Security Volunteers. The people dubbed it the "Ton-Ton Macoute"—a Creole expression meaning "bogeymen." This organization soon became known for its cruelty. Antagonistic labor leaders and troublesome intellectuals were imprisoned and tortured, some even murdered, by the bogeymen. The volunteers were behind the expulsion of Archbishop François Poirier, Catholic primate of Haiti. Duvalier himself was excommunicated, a meaningless gesture since he was a total voodooist. Actually, Catholicism itself was rather meaningless in Haiti.

In any event, the bogeymen spread through Haiti like a disease. Nobody was safe. A peasant on a lonely trail in the Haitian hills was asked what he thought of Duvalier. Stiffening at the question, he looked about at the silent trees. "Espion," he said. "Espion everywhere . . ."

At the dinner table in a private house an English planter referred to "the head man." Someone wanted to know who he meant. Almost inaudibly he whispered, "Duvalier," and then pointed to his kitchen where the houseboy was washing dishes. "TTM," he warned, using the common abbreviation for the bogeymen.

In Port-au-Prince one day the wife of a famous American foreign correspondent had gone shopping with a Haitian friend. At noon they had arranged to meet the journalist on a street corner, but he was late. "I hope that man Duvalier hasn't shot my husband," the white woman said jokingly. She turned to see the Haitian friend scuttling into the nearest doorway.

Inevitably, the Ton-Ton Macoute became a law unto itself and Duvalier was obliged to let the bogeymen ransack the country at will. Their specialty, like Al Capone's, was extortion. Plantation owners and businessmen had to pay heavily for "insurance" and were forced to pad their payrolls with so-called guards and nightwatchmen. The lame-duck U.S. foreign-aid mission was the easiest touch. The work force for one project numbered thirty, although the record showed that six hundred were actually on the payroll. The owner of a banana plantation who had refused to hire guards woke up one morning to find half his crop stripped from the trees. A young engineer, who helped build the Peligre Dam and who had established tourist cottages on the banks as a private enterprise, returned from a vacation to find that bogeymen had taken over his business. There was nothing he could do about it.

With the example set by the TTM, government grafters became increasingly blatant in their own shakedowns. An American firm wanting to plant crops in the Artibonite Valley had to contribute twenty thousand dollars before the first seed was sown. An oil company was asked for five thousand dollars. When the money was not forthcoming, the demand was upped to seven and a half thousand. There was still no reply, so the company was ordered to pay ten thousand within forty-eight hours or get out of Haiti. The check duly arrived.

The most deplorable situation of all faced young Haitian doctors doing their mandatory two-year residencies in country hospitals. Their regular monthly checks of one hundred dollars, intended for both salary and the running expenses of the twenty-bed clinics, were cut to eighty dollars. "It's to help fix the budget" was the explanation from Port-au-Prince.

One young doctor, haggard after seeing ninety patients between dawn and dusk, said he had no linen, medicines, or staff. He was counting the weeks until his residency finished so he could leave Haiti and join his five hundred colleagues already abroad. Fifty doctors had graduated that year in Port-au-Prince. The country would be lucky to keep ten of them. One doctor to two thousand people is supposed to be the bare minimum to keep a country reasonably healthy. In Haiti, the ratio was one to ten thousand.

Most honest Haitians with a special skill deserted the republic if they had the chance. Self-respect was hard to sustain amid so much general deterioration. Yet somehow it was sustained by thousands of ignorant working men obliged to stay on. Their prideful gestures were pathetic.

There was the story of a family man in Port-au-Prince earning fifty cents a day, who wore rags and ate garbage to save a few coins each week. At the end of a year he walked into a store, plunked down eight dollars, and bought himself a beautiful new white shirt. Casually, as if he were accustomed to fine clothes, he wore the shirt to work next day and pretended not to notice envious, curious looks from his friends. When the boss came by and rubbed the material between his thumb and forefinger admiringly, the man thrust out his bottom lip thoughtfully. "Not a bad shirt," he said. "Cost me fourteen dollars."

The boss knew the man was exaggerating the price, but he did not comment. "With that shirt," he said later, "the fellow's saying to the world, 'I'm still an individual, the master of my fate.' You see, the shirt is his badge of distinction. I've known men to starve until they save up five dollars for a really good prostitute. They remember their time with her in every detail and talk about it for the rest of their lives. It is an experience that sets them apart from other poor men."

The tragic hopelessness of the peasants was repeated throughout Haiti in the late fifties and early sixties. The only exception, at least for a while, was in the Artibonite Valley. The ODVA survived as Duvalier's showcase project. Chuck Wiggin was brought back on the job; under his direction the irrigation channels were pushed far across the valley and a big rice mill was constructed. A certain leakage of ODVA funds in Port-au-Prince was apparent, but Wiggin prayed it would not get too bad before the irrigation scheme became self-supporting. Once a dairy farmer in New Hampshire, Wiggin loved to look at fat brown cows grazing thick green grass; he wanted this lushness for the Artibonite region.

Peasants cheered when the brown water first began to trickle through the fields, not all of which belonged to peasants, to be sure. The government still claimed a wide acreage in the valley as its own. But at least the water had arrived. Even though the peasants distrusted any enterprise connected with the government, they felt hopeful now that everyone would get irrigation.

New vegetable gardens and rice paddies were established; bumper harvests attracted thousands of Haitians to the valley to look for work. Although property owners paid only around thirty-five cents a day and a meal, on the ODVA tracts unskilled workers were making close to real wealth—a dollar a day. Peasants whose *cailles* lay in the path of a projected canal were compensated as much as two hundred dollars just for a house. This, too, was welcome money, since the owners could dismantle the house and move it to another spot. Lucky farmers with three acres of land in the irrigated section, changing from sugar cane to rice, doubled their incomes to four hundred dollars a year. More people could afford to clothe their children and replace the straw roofs on their huts with galvanized iron.

Slowly, slowly, the Artibonite was becoming green. Wiggin, seeing such a tremendous difference, encouraged white planters to invest in the area. A Scotsman put in a big fiber crop, and a man from Georgia seeded an experimental field with tobacco. But Wiggin had second thoughts about the sincerity of their faith in the Artibonite region when the Scot reminded him that the Haitians were the cheapest labor available in the Americas and the Georgian balked at paying his men twelve- and- a- half cents an hour on a Sunday instead of the usual dime.

In a few more years, thought Wiggin, the valley will be fully reclaimed and there will be first-class foreign investment here. He was to be denied his "few" years.

USAID dried up just when it was most needed—at the point in the irrigation plan where most of the land was ready and waiting for the final transformation. After ignoring graft for so long, Washington suddenly stopped all aid, even though another million or two would have made the whole rotten episode worthwhile. Duvalier had piqued Washington by running a phony ballot and getting himself "elected" for another six-year term. Even so, the money would have been resumed if he had allowed USAID men to watchdog future expenditures and if he had curbed the extortion practices of the TTM. His hands were tied, however. Duvalier was trapped now within his own power complex.

Thus, the historic combination of Port-au-Prince greed and foreign indifference killed the dreams of a quarter million peasants. ODVA's target date for a rejuvenated Artibonite—1962—became the year when the project died. The big yellow bulldozers were left to rust in the fields, the bogeymen stole the trucks, the irrigation channels started to clog up with grass and reeds, and a heartbroken Chuck Wiggin left for Bolivia on a new assignment.

Mellon alone seems to understand how useless and demeaning it is to give handouts to Haiti or any other backward country on the condition that it behave itself. For one thing, behavior is always judged from the viewpoint of the rich country. There is no altruism in this system and no security. It invites violation.

Mellon's gift was primarily a gift of self. His money could easily have come to naught in Haiti if he had not given himself as well. His unselfishness was its own protection. Bogeymen did not trouble him, and a shake-down was tried only once.

Inspired by the climate of graft, the director of the free cemetery at Verrettes decided he was getting so many bodies from Deschapelles that he would charge Mellon five gourdes in the future for every corpse brought in for burial. Mellon said he would not pay but he would send men from the hospital to bury the bodies. The next day Mellon himself and the Deschapelles padre, the Reverend Joseph Bois, drove up with three dead men in a truck. The white man and the black man stripped to the waist and started to dig a grave in the hard soil. By midday, having finished only one grave, they were utterly exhausted. With a prayer of apology they tipped all three bodies in the one grave and filled it in. Meanwhile, the cemetery man had been sitting under a tree, smoking one cigarette after another. He was almost weeping with shame when Mellon left. Never again did he ask for burial money.

Beholden to no one and relying on no one, Mellon went

about his work with inscrutable simplicity. "A pussyfoot," one American in the valley called him. "A softie who's just making trouble for himself. When the Haitians are ready, they'll screw him but good."

Many people saw a hidden threat in the widely quoted exchange between the doctor and the president at a capital function. Mellon reminded Duvalier that he had not yet visited the hospital.

"That's true," said Duvalier. "But I know everything that's happening there."

One day a summons arrived from the presidential palace. Larry and Gwen Mellon and several of the Haitian staff drove to town to answer it. In an ornate ceremony, Mellon was presented with a medal for his services to Haiti.

All doubts about how far Mellon would go to safeguard his operation in Haiti were removed by his treatment of the zealous young vet who replaced Julian Strauss. This man soon became engrossed in the pig project and sought to improve it.

Hospital trucks were being used to cart the marketable "parlor" pigs to Port-au-Prince for sale, but the new vet thought the porkers were losing too much weight on the long, hot trip. Why not slaughter them at the hospital and truck the carcasses? The vet proposed the idea to Mellon.

Unfortunately, said the boss, the law restricted the slaughter of animals for market to the Haitian American Meat Company. The vet checked around and discovered that although this law was on the books many other companies and individuals ignored it and slaughtered away as they pleased.

Good enough, he decided. When the next lot of pigs were

collected and brought to the hospital, he had them slaughtered then and there. The next morning at five, a special truck was to come from Saint Marc to take the carcasses to market. The vet went to bed early so as to rise at dawn.

Meanwhile Mellon, who had been away for a few days, returned that evening to find the hospital's cold-storage chamber full of pig carcasses. When he heard the story, he canceled the truck from Saint Marc and went to bed in a cold fury. The poor young vet faced that fury the next morning.

"I'll see you at the hospital at eight," Mellon curtly told him when he appeared at the house. And at eight o'clock the boss had the young man on the carpet, asking why he had decided to break the law in the name of the hospital.

"It's not really breaking the law," said the vet. "Others do it all the time." Mellon's face reddened and tears came to his eyes. He fired the man on the spot.

In a small community like Deschapelles, this was a first-class scandal. For months doctors and nurses argued the justice of the case. One doctor almost resigned in sympathy. Meanwhile the vet asked for another chance, and, because he was an extremely popular young man, even the peasants spoke up on his behalf.

The boss, however, remained adamant, so the crestfallen boy left Deschapelles. To Mellon's mind there was no alternative. He could not afford to take a chance on an indiscreet staff member when the survival of villages like Estrale, the very existence of hundreds of families in community development projects, and the life of the hospital itself were at stake.

NOW PAST FIFTY, Larry Mellon sometimes acted like a man in a hurry. He gave himself another twenty or twenty-five years to keep developing the hospital and his various community projects. By then, he figured, he might be dead. A frown would cross his face; he feared that the hospital might die with him.

"Our job," he repeated, as he had said earlier, "is to stimulate the Haitians to take an interest in their own hospital because eventually we want to turn the whole thing over to them."

By "stimulate," Mellon meant to build a sense of responsibility in the Haitians for each other's welfare. He sought to do this by Christian example, or just plain brotherly love.

"Dr. Mellon does not preach the Gospel, he practices it," said Pastor Bois. "You might say he preaches by example. This seems to me the most valuable way to serve Christ. Even if many Haitians in the valley are too ignorant to want to share in Dr. Mellon's work, in their hearts they know that he is a good man and helping them. If I were as spiritually deep as Dr. Mellon, I'd regard myself as a perfect man."

But in spite of what Pastor Bois said about the Haitians'

appreciation of Mellon, the man, most peasants had a blind spot about altruism and social responsibility. This was understandable; they lived under military law and had no say whatever in the government. Instead of tribal chiefs as in the old Africa, Haiti had paternal, disciplinary chefs-de-section—district civil officers serving the army posts. The servile peasants minded their own business and concentrated on staying alive and keeping peace with the voodoo gods.

At first Mellon had expected much from Haitian professional men and skilled workers, but often he was disappointed. One white employee at the hospital stated the situation bluntly: "The Haitian interest in the hospital starts and ends with the fortnightly pay check."

And so Mellon considered it a major victory when Dr. Pierre Sterlin, Jerome Jean-Baptiste, and other Haitians on his staff announced one day that they were pooling their savings to build a TB village. Although Mellon had never doubted the kindness of his top men, he was taken by surprise now. Nothing, however, was needed more desperately. Pulmonary tuberculosis had reached such epidemic proportions in the valley that it could not be curbed. The few beds in the hospital's isolation ward were pitifully inadequate. A quarantined village, humble or not, would be far superior.

L'Escale, as the new village was called, quickly took shape on a knoll a quarter mile from the hospital.

Just the buying of the land had cut deeply into the slim budget, so construction was limited at first to two concrete four-bedroom houses, each costing seven hundred and fifty dollars. Soon, however, two more houses were financed by Tom White, a Tennessee physician returning to practice in the States. A kitchen was added, and the first patients were taken into L'Escale.

Apart from White's gift, the only stroke of good fortune was the presence of a Haitian matron named Louise who was hired to cook and clean for the TB patients. Taking pride in having her own personal village, she equipped it with a garden of maize, corn, cotton bushes, and melons. She further reduced the heavy food bills by raising chickens and ducks. The running expenses of L'Escale, more than two hundred dollars a month, were met by Haitians on the hospital staff. That was all they could afford, so L'Escale had scant hope of expanding for some time.

Someone now suggested that patients should earn money for the village by working at simple crafts. This came to little, however. Rope-making proved to be too strenuous for people with TB. Some patients made excellent necklaces from jequirity seeds, but the project stopped after children chewed the beads and came down with mild cases of poisoning.

Tiny L'Escale required great personal sacrifice from the Haitians involved. Because of Mellon's example, however, they did not give up, although several were close to despair—among them René St. Léger, the superb and explosive Haitian physician. He was on twenty-four-hour call for the village, as well as for his regular clinic work in the Hôpital Albert Schweitzer.

"We get more than a thousand patients with pulmonary tuberculosis at Deschapelles every year," St. Léger said. "They flock here from all over Haiti, because, except for one sanitarium near Port-au-Prince, they have nowhere else to go. We can take eighteen patients at L'Escale, but even these few are not always the right ones. We want people who may recover rapidly, yet we are forced to accept advanced cases as well. Some of them are so bad they'd die on the long journey home. We simply have to take them in.

"What can we accomplish with only eighteen beds when ten per cent of Haiti's population has tuberculosis? That's around four hundred thousand people. Most of the peasants who come here are given drugs and sent home. That is—if they still have a home. Peasants know enough about TB now to be scared to death of it. A person with pulmonary tuberculosis is told not to share his utensils and to use a mask if he is around other people. Yet if he follows these instructions the others know he has *malade toussé,* disease of the cough, and they won't have anything to do with him. There is a sixteen-year-old girl here disowned by her family and ostracized for fear she'd contaminate her brothers and sisters. So many TB cases don't admit to the disease and don't take the necessary precautions. As a result, whole families are stricken. TB is spreading every day."

St. Léger paused to light a cigarette. His eyes shone with anger.

"Have you ever sent a man with tuberculosis home to his wife and kids? Well, the first time you feel very sorry. Then you have to do it a second time, and you're just a little less sorry because you've done it before and you know there's no alternative. So you go on doing it, again and again. By the hundredth time you feel nothing. You've become a monster."

St. Léger is the archetypal educated Haitian Negro, impatient and impassioned. Some day the future of Deschapelles may be in the hands of a man like him. A St. Léger would not conduct a guerilla action against disease; he would wage a full frontal attack in an all-or-nothing campaign.

"The sisters tell me I'm doing God's work so I should be content," St. Léger said quietly. "I say to them that it's okay to do something for God, but a man like me must do something for himself, too. I must work to a plan and feel that I'm accomplishing something. If my job is to pile one stone on top of another stone, then, finally, I want to see a building. I don't want to pile stones for nothing. But that's what I'm doing here."

With Mellon, self has never been a consideration. He is, in fact, committed to spending himself little by little in tortuous chipping away at the sky-high barrier to a complete solution of Haitian problems. But he could remind St. Léger that L'Escale did exist and was already performing a good service. So here again, a beginning had been made. Now ODVA houses were being vacated; perhaps in time L'Escale could take them over and become a great sanitarium. In any event, one had to keep whittling at a stupendous problem until it was merely a big task. L'Escale was not just a glancing blow at the mammoth TB problem; it was a good solid cut.

Similarly, Pastor Bois had made a humble though worthy start in caring for the many homeless waifs of Haiti. The padre's main duty at the hospital was to deliver to their homes by station wagon both the very old and the very young patients. This was a tough assignment so far as the youngsters were concerned; their listed addresses gave only the name of a village or district. The padre often spent an entire day with one child, driving across the valley and up into the hills, looking for parents or relatives. Occasionally mothers and fathers left their homes without trace. When this happened, Pastor Bois had to find foster parents or place the deserted children in the care of hospital nurses who might use them as servants.

Of all the people at Deschapelles, Pastor Bois reserved his highest regard for Larry Mellon. The grave-digging incident, he said, was the best lesson of his life in "how to be a chief." If something had to be done, do it yourself.

Haitian orphans required a home, so he decided to build one. The padre was a poor man, but he managed to scrape together twenty dollars a month for his special orphanage fund. In two years he had five hundred dollars, enough to lease a small piece of land down the road from the hospital and to begin building. Although he planned initial accommodation for only twelve children, Pastor Bois ran out of money before the bedrooms were furnished with cots and even before the roof was on. His capital had vanished even though he had laid the foundations himself and raised the walls with his own two hands.

The padre, however, had such complete faith in the power of prayer that he did not worry for a second. Kneeling in his pink-walled orphanage under the open sky, he asked God's help. Shortly after this, Mellon came by and offered him spare roofing timbers and iron. Then a New Yorker, told about the little orphanage in a letter, mailed the padre a check for a hundred dollars. Soon other checks started to arrive, and the orphanage was opened.

One of the first patients was a boy of ten taken there after his leg had been amputated and his parents had refused to keep him at home; Gwen Mellon paid for this boy herself. Another boy's parents had died while he was in the hospital.

And Yolande, the youngest of the twelve orphans, had been dumped on the hospital steps one night.

The foster mother for the children was a peasant girl of twenty-one who had come to St. Léger's clinic in a state of acute depression. Destitute, she had been existing on whatever she could pick up in the fields. To St. Léger medicine did not mean solely drugs. He prescribed for her the human companionship and the sense of being wanted that the orphanage could provide. Pastor Bois agreed that the girl's spirit needed healing more than her body. The experiment was a gamble that paid off. Yolande called the girl "Mama," and after a time, the young woman stopped correcting the child.

More people at Deschapelles were concerned now about the lack of money for carrying on all the various projects planned for the peasants. Mellon was obviously short of funds. Half his budget was made up of five and ten dollar checks from all over the world, mostly contributions from word-of-mouth advertising, for right up into the sixties only a few short magazine articles had been written about the Hôpital Albert Schweitzer. Expenses increased faster than the donations; Mellon found himself going into the red. As a result, he cut back on gifts of medicine to other Haitian clinics and his staff was tougher in screening out-district patients. Also, in this emergency other doctors on his team tried to assume some of the financial burden of expansion.

Harold May, for instance, was an enthusiastic lay preacher as well as chief surgeon. He conducted Protestant services for the staff twice every Sunday in an outside wing of the hospital. He could have built a real chapel because the white worshippers had contributed generously to the collections. Instead, May and the others decided to use their money to establish a first-class elementary school.

Named École la Providence, it grew into a spacious stone structure on eight acres of land adjoining the hospital housing settlement. Soon a hundred children were studying there, and the sponsors planned to add a classroom for another thirty children each year. This, too, would be financed from church collections. In keeping with Mellon's insistence on excellence, a fine teacher to head the school was imported from Switzerland. Children were supplied with uniforms—checkered dresses for the girls and checkered shirts and navy-blue pants for the boys.

The aim was to maintain a high standard in dress, discipline, attendance, and education. A few miles away, a government primary school held four hundred children and two teachers. But here the youngsters came to school or stayed away as they pleased. Actually only a small proportion of the valley children had the chance to attend any school at all. École la Providence would not go very far toward solving the general problem, but it would serve as a model for the few schools that did exist.

Prestige seekers never sought entrance to Groton more hopefully than the Haitians did to École la Providence. Nearly a thousand parents applied for admission of their children, showing that the peasantry hungered for education as much as it did for food. Of course, this number had to be drastically reduced, so each child was given an intelligence test. Fees were eighty cents a month, but very poor parents of successful applicants were permitted to pay off their children's tuition by laboring on the school grounds four days a month.

Suzanne Depeursinge, the first Swiss directress, soon decided how the tribe of workers could best be employed. Several of the children, she found, fell asleep in school from hunger. They had eaten no breakfast. For a time, CARE food was available for school snacks; but when this gave out, only milk was supplied. To use food from Mellon's hospital for this select group of school children would have been unfair to the other youngsters in the district. So Suzanne Depeursinge decided to use parent labor and part of the school acreage for an agricultural program. Food for school meals would be grown on the spot.

But since their wages had already been paid in tuition for their children, the Haitians saw no reason for exerting themselves in the school gardens. Andy Gallagher, the hospital's cynical maintenance man, would pass by with a knowing look in his eye. Instead of dark glasses to hide behind, he thought, these guys have a hoe to lean on.

When Harold May heard of this laziness from Joe, the school's Haitian groundsman, he called a meeting of parents. "We are not fooling around at this school," he said quietly. "We expect the children to apply themselves in the classroom and we expect the parents who have agreed to work to apply themselves to their tasks. If you don't work, parents, you'll have to pay the fees. And if you don't pay the fees, your child can't come to school."

After the meeting more sweat dripped onto the black soil of École la Providence, but May was more convinced than ever that Christian ethics should be added to the school curriculum.

Although the Hôpital Albert Schweitzer was spawning several subsidiaries run by the staff under separate budgets, Mellon was careful not to relinquish control over the broad operation.

For example, several Chicago eye doctors—later to be known as the FOCUS group—wanted to establish a clinic at Deschapelles as an annex to the hospital which they would administer themselves. Mellon politely suggested they go elsewhere since he already had a splendid eye clinic. They accepted the rebuff and founded their little hospital at Port-de-Paix. Next, American research teams asked to use his hospital as a laboratory for their study of tropical diseases. Never, said Mellon, appalled at the thought of Deschapelles acquiring a "guinea-pig" label.

He did, however, incorporate his hospital in a three-way link, joining forces with Sister Joan Margaret's St. Vincent's school for handicapped children at Port-au-Prince and with Caroline Bradshaw's child convalescent-and-therapy center at La Pointe des Palmistes near Port-de-Paix.

Youngsters with rickets, tuberculosis of the bone, club feet, and other deformities of the limbs were first strengthened for corrective operations at Caroline's place. The actual surgery was then done at Deschapelles by visiting orthopedists. After that, Caroline again provided the beds for the recuperating children. And when they were well enough, they were taken to St. Vincent's for schooling.

Caroline—"Miss Caro" to the Haitians—was a doughty servant of the Unevangelized Fields Mission (undenominational, but following Baptist doctrine). A gay, unsinkable woman in her forties, she barged from one end of Haiti to the other in a station wagon called "Elizabeth." It was perpetually full of children, twisted in body but happy in spirit. They watched and listened with delight as their female Friar Tuck rattled over the bumps with a whoop of joy, calling, "Come on, boys and girls, let's sing . . ." Her voice rang over the roar of the engine and echoed down the lonely roads:

> This world is not my home
> I'm just a-travelin' through . . .

Caroline brought sparkle to Deschapelles. She flashed in and out of the place in a shapeless dress and dusty shoes, daring to say and do things that shocked the narrowly pious. Caroline bowed before no one except God, and she seemed to be in His good graces.

"Some day I'm going to write a book and call it *God Always Knows When to Put a Rock Behind the Wheel,*" she said. "Elizabeth was stalled on a hill once. The gear wouldn't hold her, the hand brake was gone, and I had to keep my foot on the pedal. I was trapped, unable to get out to see what was wrong. If only I could put a rock behind the wheel, I thought. At that moment a little boy popped up from nowhere and said to me, 'Hey, do you want me to put a rock behind the wheel?' This happens to me all the time. Every day of my life is a miracle."

Next to Mellon, no American in Haiti had accomplished more than Caroline, and now she was adding her magic to his.

She first reached the island from Newport News in 1943, setting herself up as a missionary midwife in a palm-leaf shelter located in the northern hills. And over the years, despite extreme privation and a series of illnesses, Caroline delivered about thirteen hundred babies. The mission station gradually expanded and she took on more general duties; her talent, however, lay in meeting impossible challenges. When Sister Joan Margaret and Mellon began to work together with handicapped children, Caroline saw a chance to help them. They needed beds for the children to convalesce after surgery. Caroline immediately offered the limited bed space available at La Pointe des Palmistes.

The demands on her mounted rapidly. Soon she needed eighty beds, not twenty. She stretched her part of the mission budget, added money of her own, solicited donations, made some hard-headed deals with Haitian construction men, and ended up in 1962 with an eighty-bed clinic—La Maison d'Espoir. How she ever paid for it she can't recall; nor can she remember now how she kept it going. Her budget was only sufficient to cover the expenses for half the children. Since La Maison was always full, she had to rely on checks from out of the blue for the other half. Incredibly, they came. People who had heard about her work sent regular donations of ten dollars, the monthly cost of supporting one child. Then a woman in Canada sent Caroline the money for a down payment on "Elizabeth," and later paid the monthly installments.

Caroline's station-wagon trips on the rough roads between Deschapelles and La Maison became legend. When the floods came everybody stopped traveling except Miss Caro. Once, with Orthopedic Surgeon Bob Wells on board, she was halted at a swollen river. About to wade on into the torrent in search of a footing for "Elizabeth," Caroline hesitated; she wore only nylon pants underneath her dress and so many Haitians were watching.

"I'll feel very white and naked," she told Wells. "It's all right for the Haitian girls with their black legs and pretty red pants."

Wells, opening his suitcase, handed Caroline a pair of long white underpants. Attired in these, the missionary woman took to the water and soon guided "Elizabeth" to the far bank.

On another occasion she was forced to stay the night at the house of a Haitian businessman notorious for his collection of fat mistresses. Since Caroline herself was of ample size, one of her superiors chided her later for her indiscretion. "I was puzzled by his attitude," said Caroline. "I've never thought of myself as a woman."

Christian missionaries have been targets for criticism in every primitive country of the world. Often they destroy spiritual customs and fail to replace them with beliefs as strong and as comforting. Many have regarded themselves as superior—God's chosen people—and have treated the natives in a manner that was insulting. Caroline's own mission contained a person who actively disliked the Haitians because they did not seem to respect and obey white people. This missionary had worked in the Congo when the Belgians still ruled there and had found that experience much more "rewarding."

Voodoo, of course, is a complete religion and gives the peasants so much security, solace, and fun, that a missionary is morally bound to be very sure of his talents before starting to sabotage it. Unfortunately there were a number of stupid missionaries in Haiti who went right ahead, damaging without reconstructing.

Mellon has never wanted his place to be known as a missionary hospital. "To me," he insists, "religion is a means of sustaining one's self and is not to be talked about or disseminated."

Caroline would never entirely agree, but she, too, believed that example was the important thing. Whether she counted herself as a woman or not, she is one of the noblest human beings to figure in the saga of Deschapelles.

12

THESE, then, are some of the people and events that have given heart and history to a place called Deschapelles. There are very few spots like it on earth; its sole *raison d'être* is mercy and goodness.

Apart from the Haitians, not many people have been there. But those that have—mostly the doctors and nurses—remember it often, and sometimes they return. They go back to regain their perspective, to be refreshed. Nobody paints it as a Lourdes or even a Lambaréné, but Deschapelles is, in its way, a sanctuary from the tawdriness, pettifoggery, and vanity of the commercial world.

At dusk, when the sun has stopped glaring out of the sky and the air is sweet and the hubbub of another clinic day has hushed, Deschapelles is a delicious place. This is the time of the lull. The men and women who walk along the paths under the trees close their eyes to feel it. They have used the day, every moment of it, to do their utmost to help and heal other men. They have earned the cool serenity and peace of the dusk.

The creation of Deschapelles has been Larry Mellon's proudest achievement, but Gwen Mellon has been his constant companion and major domo. Neither has cared that the peasants have often confused their roles right from the start.

Mellon was driving near Verrettes one day when he saw four men carrying a prostrate peasant on a door. He stopped the car and hurried over to the sick man.

"Do you mind if I examine him?" Mellon asked. The man plainly had a gangrenous leg.

"We're taking him to Madame Mellon's hospital," said one of the bearers, as the four kept on walking.

"Well, I know Madame Mellon pretty well," said Mellon. "She's my wife. Come on now, let me have a look at that leg."

The four men shrugged and put down their burden. "Okay, *blanc,*" they said.

This incident and others like it—which Mellon loved to relate—showed that Gwen had made the stronger impression in the valley among many people. She enjoyed, to be sure, the boss role of taking peasants' money on clinic days, but there was more to it than that. Mellon was self-effacing, apparently too meek and artless to be top man. When the hospital was being built and the doctor was laboring with a cement-mixer, even Caroline had once mistaken him for one of the hired hands. A friend of Pastor Bois, who had seen Mellon, grubby and disheveled, wrestling with cotton drapes and dye vats, refused to believe he was the head of the entire hospital.

Even some white members of the staff regarded Gwen Mellon as the more formidable partner. An added reason for this was that Mellon had detached himself from the hospital's social life. He was always out in the valley, absorbed with peasant problems; little of himself was left over for other interests. This preoccupation sometimes even closed him off from his own family. "He can be great fun to be with," said his stepdaughter Jenny. "But there are times when you can't make contact at all."

Meeting Mellon for the first time, many think him shy, but, as Jenny sees it, "He doesn't have enough self-concern to be shy."

Family, friends and staff members went then—and still do—to Gwen Mellon for advice. Although most of those at Deschapelles call her "Madame" Mellon—a formality she does not discourage—she has always been more gregarious than her husband, more available. She has become the arbiter of personal disputes, enforcer of discipline, and preserver of the esprit de corps.

"I don't think the hospital would keep functioning without Gwen," said one doctor, suggesting that this is indeed a case of the "woman behind the man."

In reality, it is probably the other way around. Gwen both loves and admires her husband and understands the force of his dedication. To her he is an heroic figure. Whatever she does as chief personnel officer, she does because Mellon would do the same thing. In her actions, however, Gwen is more assertive than her husband. Hence she is considered the dominant personality. The two actually complement each other beautifully.

Gwen has always been devoted to the hospital her husband built. At one time she was gravely ill for seven weeks. The doctors at Deschapelles could not figure out what was wrong, and her weight went down to about a hundred pounds. Yet she chose to rely on the medical talents of the Hôpital Albert Schweitzer and refused to be taken to the States.

Then, after a night of crisis during which Mellon thought Gwen was going to die, he drove her to Port-au-Prince and asked his medical director, Dr. Robert Hollister, to escort her on the plane to New York. Hollister had been going to Chicago anyway. A week of special treatment at Medical Center's Harkness Pavilion did not improve Gwen's condition. A visitor found her painfully thin and panting for breath. Yet there was a faint smile on her lips.

"They couldn't find anything more about my trouble here than the doctors could at Deschapelles," she whispered. "That makes me very proud." These might have been her dying words if specialists had not later decided she was being weakened by a blood clot. After appropriate treatment, she recovered.

But when Gwen Mellon is at her best, she uses to its fullest every second of the day. With her orderly mind and great capacity for work, she is never comfortable simply sitting and talking. Visitors to Deschapelles, no matter how distinguished, could rarely find Mellon, and if they were willing to settle for a conversation with Gwen, they might have to do so above the chatter of her sewing machine. On clinic days one followed her from the registration desk to the baby clinic, to the wards, or to anywhere else she had things to do. Deschapelles was a world set apart, not to be interrupted by any circumstance. All that counted there were the peasants' needs, this hour, this minute. Nothing was allowed to distract from this purpose.

The Mellons took only one vacation a year—to New York to see their family. None of the children had chosen Deschapelles as a home. Jenny was a housewife in New Jersey, Ian was a teacher, Mike was off wandering in Europe. Billy Mellon, who had been studying medicine, died tragically in 1963.

Despite this lack of family contact for most of the year, the Mellons did not think they were making a sacrifice. Nothing about their lives in Haiti counted as self-denial to them. They felt they had gained a great deal more than they had given up in going there.

A doctor's wife once asked Mellon why he did not get away more and relax.

"You don't understand," he said. "This is where I like to be all the time. Who needs a vacation from paradise?"

Mellon is somewhat inclined to emphatic statements like this, but I have no doubt he meant it. Eager to see his part of Haiti as he himself saw it, I moved further out into the hinterland—into the bosom of the peasantry—where the whole scene was not so overshadowed by the suffering at the hospital. Mellon had spent most of the previous four years in this area and had been charmed beyond recall.

One day, during my visit in October, 1962, I recruited a peasant guide and rode on horseback for six hours far into the hills to a place called Terre Nette. It was at the extreme end of the hospital district. We climbed into the sun with the silver water tower at the hospital long visible behind. Our little horses scuttled and stumbled along deep rutted paths in the rock face of the hills. In places there was room for only one horse to pass and we had to rein our mounts onto the shoulder of the trail and balance there while the downcoming traffic passed. Women, mainly, were on their way to markets in the valley. Some walked with baskets of citrus and ground corn on their heads. Others were astride burros heavily packed with sugar cane, grains, and firewood.

My guide, Eliani, a young man of gusto, greeted everyone

with a happy *"bo'jour"* and engaged in badinage with several. A woman who knew that Eliani worked on Mellon's community development team boldly demanded some building timber. "Of course," said Eliani. "I'll speak to the president about it." They went their separate ways, both giggling at Eliani's wit.

The hillsides had been stripped of native trees and bushes generations before and were now badly eroded. There were areas, however, where some top soil remained. Grass grew thick and green here, and contoured plots of beans and potatoes flourished. The plateaus were still reasonably fertile and rippled with fields of maize. But where a natural tropic garden had flourished long ago, there remained only remnants, an occasional saucer of ground where the soil was held fast and where royal palms and banana trees grew in profusion.

We crossed one row of hills and then another, moving higher and higher until the entire Artibonite Valley was spread below. Coiling across its floor was the brown river, in places almost bending back on itself. Petite Rivière showed up as a smudge in the center of the valley. This was the important town for the three hundred thousand peasants living in this wedge of Haiti. Its stone buildings went back to the days of the slavers and bore the scars of battle from the Haitian war of independence fought a century and a half before the Negroes in Africa gained the right to govern themselves.

The climb was steeper now and often we had to dismount and lead the horses. My shoes were soon chipped and torn, although I noticed that the Haitians traveled this route in bare feet without injury. Their hearts, lungs, and muscles were equally hardened. Women going our way, even pregnant women with loads on their heads, glistened all over with sweat, but did not pause to rest. Yet when I walked any distance up those hills, my heart thudded and I could barely put one leg in front of the other.

Struggling up one incline, my throat burning with thirst, we were stopped by a bright middle-aged woman carrying on her head a basket of oranges.

"Ah, Docteur," she greeted me with a wide smile. Then, after giving a little speech in Creole, which I could not understand, she reached into her basket and gave me two small green oranges. She handed two more to Eliani.

A gift to strangers of four oranges was extremely generous. Judging by her worn clothes and her lack of a horse or burro, the woman must have been very poor. I reached into my pocket to find some coins, but Eliani stopped me.

"She would be offended," he said in English. "She's been to the hospital and she thinks you're a doctor. She said she loved you and wanted to give you something."

I thanked the woman and she went off merrily down the trail.

A moment later Eliani and I mounted, and as the horses picked their way onward, we sucked the oranges. In all my life I have never tasted sweeter fruit.

Terre Nette was nothing more than a high, round hill, the topmost point of the range visible from the hospital. We tethered our horses at the base and scrambled to the top on foot. I tried to forget my failing legs by thinking of the people I had met from this remote region.

One of these was Delitane, a girl of seven now under Caroline's care. Both her feet had been eaten off by gangrene. Then there were the Meriluses, mother and son. The father had died at the hospital of pulmonary TB and friends had carried home with the body the message that Madame Merilus and young Joseph must also visit the hospital for check-ups. I saw them arriving at Deschapelles, riding one horse, the son holding his mother in front of him. Her head lolled back on his chest and he himself was at the end of his endurance. When I raised my camera to take their picture, the young man looked at me without a trace of expression, then turned away. I lowered the camera and felt like apologizing. Both, of course, had been found to have TB—Joseph in such condition that he had to be admitted.

On a shelf of land near the summit of the round hill we came to a *caille* in a grove of trees. This was Julie's house and as far as we were going. Julie was a former concubine who lived here with her mother and three children. The man who had set her up here for the pleasure of her company on weekends had since died. Now everything was Julie's—the hut, a few banana trees, coffee bushes, and an orange tree heavy with fruit. When we arrived, Julie, a gay and robust woman of twenty-four, was pounding corn into flour. She listened to Eliani's introductions, smiled at me, and showed us into the parlor of her thatched hut. From the back room she brought two chairs and set them on the dirt floor so that we could sit down. Then she took a straw basket to the orange tree and returned with a dozen oranges for our lunch.

This time I insisted on paying, but could find only one American quarter. Julie politely declined it. She said a friend had tried to use such a coin at the market and it was unacceptable to anyone.

For my own lunch I had brought two ham sandwiches, so I pulled these out of my pocket and offered them to Julie. It was not a grand gesture. I felt so dehydrated and exhausted that all I wanted was to suck oranges. Julie took the sandwiches and also my last nine cigarettes. Then, putting her loot to one side, she went back to whacking a heap of corn with a mallet.

While Eliani swapped jokes with her, I munched oranges and looked about the room. In a small open closet I could see her spare clothes neatly draped over a rope strung between two pieces of timber. Otherwise the place was bare except for our chairs and a wooden table against the wall. On the table was a green plastic cloth with prints of birds all over it. The table held a huge enamel mug, three or four drinking glasses, a pencil, and some schoolbooks. Eliani said Julie's oldest son had stayed for a time with friends in Verrettes and had gone to school there.

Before we left, Julie proudly showed me a bottle of vitamins from the Hôpital Albert Schweitzer. Then she rounded up her three sturdy youngsters and, by pointing first at them and then at the bottle, she explained that the vitamins were responsible for the health of her children.

Heading down the hills for home, I decided that Julie had a near perfect life. She lacked a man, but she had a fine family and a pocket-handkerchief Garden of Eden to call her own. I also imagined her after we had gone, sitting down to lunch, eating a ham sandwich and sipping a cup of coffee while she smoked a Lucky Strike. It would have been a lunch like that of a thousand career girls in New York. But how many career girls could reach into a tree and pick a fresh yellow banana with which to finish off the meal?

I returned to Port-au-Prince a few days later. It was a Saturday, and with Bernard Diederich, the *Time-Life* correspondent who is one of the bravest and most respected newspapermen in the Caribbean, I listened to radio bulletins. Diederich, a New Zealander, had married a beautiful Haitian girl; he adored his adopted country. Later he was banished by Duvalier because he kept writing the truth without regard for personal consequences.

He had, so he told me now, been having a busy time of it. It was the high week of the Cuban crisis, when President Kennedy had quarantined the island with destroyers and warplanes because Russia had loaded the place with missiles. But Khrushchev had backed down to the extent of offering to disarm Cuba if the United States left Guantanamo.

"War doesn't look quite so close," said Bernard. "But it sure was a week. And you were up there in the wilds and missed the lot."

I, too, was a newspaper correspondent, yet I wondered whether in the long run my story about the waging of peace and mercy would not be more memorable than the Cuban uproar. Still, Haiti was in the blockade area and I was on the spot—I should contact my office in New York. I thought it over: the cold war lost.

"How do I get out to Deschapelles without a car?" I asked Bernard. By this time I had turned in my rented car.

"Camion," said Bernard. "You can take one tomorrow morning."

The *camion,* or native bus, for Deschapelles leaves from the Texaco gas station at the edge of the putrid slums of Port-au-Prince. None of the doctors arriving for duty at the Hôpital Albert Schweitzer takes it; they are met at the airport with a car or they pay twenty-five dollars and travel up-country by taxi. The *camion* is for the peasants, who consider the dollar fare exorbitant, and for any newcomer who wants a quick introduction to the country.

Haiti proper starts at that bus terminal, suddenly and with nothing held back. A clamor of black people shout and mill about the buses. Drivers surround the travelers, pleading for their business. Shuffling hags tenaciously peddle baskets of food. A naked boy runs by chasing a pig. Two men tease a leashed fighting cock. An old Plymouth jerks to a stop and a tired mulatto girl is unloaded by five big Negroes.

Across the road are the slums, tiny hovels built of scraps of wood and iron, all squeezed together. Rain has fallen and the ground is a thick ooze partly mud and partly human and animal feces. The swarm of people scavenge the offal of the city to stay alive and even have a market for rotten fruit and vegetables. Yet there is life in these fetid slums; a life that seeks not to escape but just to get something to eat before sundown.

Incongruously modern beside the slums, the Texaco gas station is sterile-looking with new pumps, a glass-walled office, and a wide apron of smooth concrete. The bus drivers adopted the station as their Port-au-Prince terminal because it is close to the paved road running north and south. From early in the morning the concrete is alive with buses, smells, noises, and barefooted women and children toting on their heads trays of bread and candy.

That next morning I made my way to a bus that I hoped was bound for Deschapelles. Five other drivers wanted to take me, but I knew that only one bus actually went there.

Deschapelles is not on the map, but the name is known everywhere in Haiti. Perhaps just mention of it rated me a seat in the front, the most comfortable place to ride. The driver waited more than two hours—until every available inch of space was taken—before leaving.

Then we were off on the road that swept around the bay of Port-au-Prince, heading along the coast to Montrouis and Saint Marc. On one side of the first stretch a sere plain rose to brown-red, gaunt hills, while the flat blue Caribbean stretched off to the horizon on the other side. At every village of white-and-pink-washed huts the driver slowed down with horn honking. At one place he was flagged by a Haitian who walked from the dowdiest hut in a spotless white shirt, pressed pants, and gleaming shoes. Somehow he, too, fitted into the packed bus.

Stops were frequent and each time the driver turned off the engine. The starter motor sounded more and more reluctant. The battery will go dead, I thought. And it did.

Passengers climbed out briefly to ease aching muscles and some of the women lifted their skirts and squatted on the side of the road to relieve themselves. The earthiness of the Haitians brought to life everything I had ever read about the country. I remembered a passage from a novel called *Canape-Vert* by the Haitian writing team of Philippe Thoby-Marcelin and Pierre Marcelin. Introducing one character, a rowdy and a thief, they wrote: "He came into the world on the big road, in the heights of Lalue, one morning when his mother was on her way to town; the labor pains had surprised her at the end of seven months. When, as she screamed with all her might, people arrived to help her, Cius was already out, hanging by his umbilical cord—for she had given birth to him standing up . . ."

When they finished their toilet, these strong-hipped mothers of Cius helped push our bus to an incline. But the first time it did not gather enough speed to start in gear. With a disgusted air, the co-driver and, apparently, mechanic—every bus had one—got out and made a great show of propping open the hood with a stick. The passengers looked on with respect. Now the bus would certainly go. And, by fortunate accident, it actually started on the next downhill run.

Three or four times along the way we had to stop so the driver could pay road tolls—one of Duvalier's latest measures "to adjust the budget"—and to be inspected by the military patrols. *Blancs* in private cars were usually made to get out and submit to being searched for weapons. In the bus, however, the soldiers did not bother about me.

At length we came to Saint Marc, a peeling, shabby town with two-story wooden houses and dim shops in the middle and tin-roofed shacks crowding the side streets. Although less than a hundred miles from Port-au-Prince and on the main road to Gonaïves and Cap-Haitien, Saint Marc had no hotel and nothing approaching a good restaurant.

It did, however, boast a Ton-Ton Macoute tough named Adrian. He thrust his scarred face at me through the bus window when we stopped by the market. To impress his countrymen, he began to shout and tap the pistol stuck in his belt. I told him I *parle pas Creole.* This made him even more truculent because he was trying to speak English, not Creole.

Why was I traveling in a *camion?* he wanted to know. Where was my car? To him, I was a suspicious character.

"We don't want trouble in valley," he said. "Tomorrow I see Mellon about you."

Having demonstrated his authority, Adrian went away and the bus moved on: I knew that he had no intention of seeing Mellon. By the grace of Duvalier himself, the Hôpital Albert Schweitzer was the big untouchable in Haiti.

Beyond Saint Marc the landscape became more dismal by the mile. The bus was swinging into the Artibonite Valley now and here, at this end, the ground was limestone rubble scattered with dwarf shrubs. There was not a tree in sight, not on the plain nor even in the near hills. The crumbling clay walls and ragged thatching of the huts testified to abysmal poverty.

Further inland, at the Pont Sonde crossroads and then along the road to Verrettes, I could see poignant evidence of Haiti's lost hope. Irrigation had spread this far and the country was succulent with the deep rich green of rice paddies and banana trees. But with ODVA folding up, irrigation would go no further.

After all the delays, it was late afternoon when we turned at the tree nailed with the familiar hospital signboard. The sky had clouded over, bringing an early dusk, and on that last short stretch of bumpy road heavy rain-spots splashed on to the windshield.

A few peasants in their Sunday best were still moving about the immaculate grounds of the hospital and from Harold May's little church room came a chorus of Creole voices singing hymns.

I hauled my suitcase off the bus roof, paid the driver his dollar, and walked across the lawns to the house where I was staying. From a nearby bungalow I heard the sound of a radio and the urgent voice of an American announcer. For me, it held little interest.

Then a group of peasants came near. The rain had quickened, but they did not alter their easy, casual stride. I practiced saying *bonsoir,* trying to make it sound less like "bonswar" and more like the peasants' lilting *bô-swah.*

13

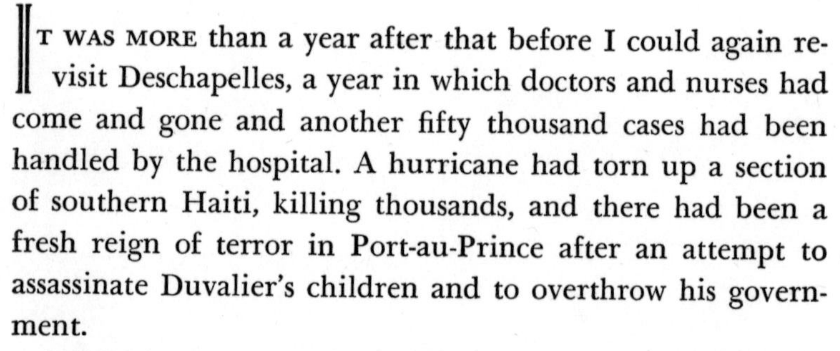

It was more than a year after that before I could again revisit Deschapelles, a year in which doctors and nurses had come and gone and another fifty thousand cases had been handled by the hospital. A hurricane had torn up a section of southern Haiti, killing thousands, and there had been a fresh reign of terror in Port-au-Prince after an attempt to assassinate Duvalier's children and to overthrow his government.

"Haiti is very sad now," Bernard Diederich had written me from Santo Domingo, his place of exile. And on the way through Jamaica, I met Bob Hamblin, a surgeon who had just left Deschapelles, who had said the same thing.

My own impression was of a Haiti more forsaken and rocked by ill fortune than ever, of Haitians as game as always, and of a Larry Mellon who was never more needed.

It was a clinic day at Deschapelles when I arrived. Distress stations had been called, and answered.

In the medical section grim-faced Bob Hollister, a big, shambling, handsome man, a missionary's son from New Berne, North Carolina, was working his way through a crush of peasants. His clothes were rumpled and one of his worn shoes was patched at the heel with white adhesive tape. Occasionally he paused in his examinations to wipe sweat from his brow with a big handkerchief. He had a habit, when tired, of tightly blinking his eyes. And on this clinic day he looked tired and older than his thirty-six years.

Back in the pediatric department, Philip Eskes, the new member of the Marshall-McGovern team, was a study in brisk professionalism. A West Indian girl named Thérèse interpreted his questions as he probed infant bodies with his fingers, depressed tongues with a wooden spatula, and examined with stethoscope and otoscope.

"This kid has a bellyache, no appetite, screams at night," droned Thérèse's flat voice. And Eskes was already writing a prescription for sulphur tablets to cure amoeba infection.

Three chairs down the line, a father grunted when his young son had an attack of diarrhea over his lap, the chair, and the floor. The father removed the child's loosely pinned diaper and mopped up the mess. Eskes looked up at the boy and dropped his pencil.

"Aw, hell," he said, "not Sam again!" It was Sam all right, released two weeks before after three months in the hospital with malnutrition and now back again with pneumonia.

Right at the end of the main corridor was the eye clinic, and the brilliant young Haitian ophthalmologist, Gérard Frédérique (Freddy), was inside exchanging jokes with an old peasant who wanted a new pair of spectacles—in fact, bifocals.

At the sight of his next patient, Freddy lost his good humor. This man complained of near blindness in one eye. Freddy checked and found fatty deposits. He cursed softly at the peasant, who dropped his eyes uncomfortably. "Syphilis," said the Haitian eye doctor.

Next door to Freddy, in the surgical clinic, Hal May and Paul Cummings, a droll young American who favored urology, were handling cases of ulcers, cancers, and hernias. On his bureau Cummings had a handbook called *Emergency War Surgery*. He must have wondered if war could put a surgeon through a more rugged trial than Deschapelles. That day he had returned from doing an emergency tracheotomy on a girl with diphtheria to find an old woman hunched up on his floor. She had been two days on the road from the Haitian Île de la Tortue. An examination revealed cancer of the cervix too far advanced to be operable. Cummings wrote a prescription for pain pills and gave her a dollar for truck fare home. "She'll be dead in three months," he said.

Nothing had changed, or could change, during those long arduous clinics—except that they had worsened.

Although the day had been hot and sunny, it was winter now and twilight brought coolness and sweetness by six o'clock. The lights came on in the hospital and in the houses too, and the cicadas announced themselves. The doctors were seeing the last of their patients. There had been four hundred of them that day. Ward beds were all occupied and ten additional cots had been spaced along the corridors. In the small overnight room, a disturbed man lay on his back, his wrists and ankles tied to the bed.

Only a few stragglers were on the steps outside the empty waiting room. A *tap-tap,* half-filled, waited in the driveway. The wide, clean stable used to tether and feed the peasant horses still contained some animals. People who had come from Terre Nette intended to sleep in the shelter and return home in the morning.

The long benchlike tables of the hospital dining room were filling up now with the medical staff, both white and Haitians, each race—surprisingly—keeping to its own tables. The Mennonites dined here; they ate quickly and with a minimum of conversation.

Most doctors had families and had been assigned houses, but at night the bachelor men and women used the cafeteria. Dr. Rachel Driver, a gentle young pediatrician recuperating from an illness, was there; also Dr. Lita Cook, a beautiful Peruvian who was relieving Lucien Rousseau, the regular anesthesiologist; Dr. Cook sat with the Haitians. Philip Eskes, whose wife and daughter were vacationing in New York, was in the cafeteria with Paul Cummings, John Nelson, and Jim Hennessey. Nelson, the semi-retired Pittsburgh dentist, was substituting for the permanent man, Pierre Verna. Hennessey, a Hartford, Connecticut, chest specialist and an old Deschapelles hand, was to replace Hollister when the medical director went on holiday.

It was a fairly typical gathering at the hospital. Somerset Maugham would have taken notes. The scene reminded me of a group of travelers stranded in a Key West hotel during a hurricane: the excitement was over; each person was subdued and alone with his private thoughts.

"Lambaréné is so different," sighed Daveka, a wide-eyed Swiss nurse who had worked there earlier. "Dr. Schweitzer would sit at a big table with the staff at supper and talk to us about everything from women's fashions to the atom bomb. We were like a family. Deschapelles isn't like that. There's nothing but misery among the peasants here. In Gabon, the Africans have plenty of food and plenty of land."

Paul Cummings shrugged and left the room. On the way out he met a nurse who said a pregnant woman had arrived in the clinic. She seemed about to give birth. Deschapelles was not a maternity hospital and Cummings disliked obstetrics. But he was on call this night and had no choice.

The woman was certainly close to delivery. She had been having pains early that morning when she first came to the hospital. Hollister had found her outside and had driven her to the government clinic at Verrettes. Apparently, however, the woman was determined to have a *blanc* bring her baby into the world, for here she was back again. Cummings put her in an empty room, examined her, and decided she would not give birth for another hour or so. Eskes, meanwhile, was in an adjoining office, setting up a blood transfusion for a little girl with malaria. He offered to keep an eye on Cummings' patient while the surgeon went to his apartment for a rest.

Thirty minutes later Cummings' telephone was ringing. It was Abel Byass, a paraplegic rescued by Mellon and put to work on the night switchboard. Emergency clinic call. Five men and a woman were in the waiting room, all groaning and clutching their stomachs.

"Happens all the time," said Cummings. "They won't wait in line during the day, so they come at night and expect immediate attention. Probably all amoeba."

The surgeon went from one to the other, asking questions in his "clinical Creole." The key word was diarrhea. Four of the men had it, and, adding this to other information, Cummings decided that the best and speediest treatment was to send them home with antacid tablets. At the sight of the pill bottles, their conditions improved instantly.

The fifth man, however, remained writhing in pain. Cummings felt his stomach. It was hard as a board.

"He can't be that good an actor," the voice crackled behind the American urologist—St. Léger had appeared in the clinic. With his better Creole, the Haitian quickly learned that the patient had not passed his bowels in a week. The doctors agreed that nature needed some drastic assistance. So Sadius Seide, aged thirty-five, was admitted to the ward.

The woman, too, was in serious trouble. She told St. Léger that she had a persistent burning thirst; ants were attracted to her urine: diabetes. Cummings called in Sam Martin, the Mennonite laboratory boss, to run a test on her blood sugar, while the woman herself was escorted down to the medical ward by Daveka, the Swiss nurse. There Daveka stripped the peasant of her ragged clothes, bathed, and dressed her in white cotton pedal pushers and smock. Sam Martin's test revealed that the woman's blood sugar was 676 milligrams when it should have been 80. By every rule of medicine, the woman should have been in a diabetic coma.

The nurses and aides, mostly Haitian, had to move about carefully now to avoid disturbing the sleeping patients in the beds along the corridors. They were an efficient team, coaxed rather than drilled to perfection by their extraordinary supervisor, Miss Pete. "If you stand over the Haitian girls all the time, they are resentful and won't do anything," she said. "So I just show them what to do and leave them." This was not Andy Gallagher's method, but it worked—at least for Miss Pete.

In the pediatric ward, thirty tetanus babies were hovering

between life and death. A nurse was feeding one of them medication through an eye-dropper. Another nurse moved among the malnutrition children with dixie cups of a Chloromycetin solution. Over several cots extended those clear, up-ended bottles of liquid food, dripping life through long plastic tubes into children's veins.

Three youngsters were to die during the night, but many more would pass the crisis and begin to regain their health. Take Victor, for instance, a three-year-old who had entered the hospital six weeks earlier in a state of starvation. Now he wandered through the ward, teasing the less sick children, his round, black bottom poking through the gap at the back of his too small hospital gown. Victor had eaten with the children, then sneaked off to the medical ward to have seconds with the adults. He had been due to leave Deschapelles a week ago, but his parents had not yet come for him. And though beds were short, the nurses were reluctant to let him go. Victor was the healthiest, sauciest little boy in Haiti; he was good for the general morale.

Paul Cummings ruffled Victor's hair as he walked past him on the way to the waiting room to find St. Léger. The Haitian was in the library reading a philosophy book by Albert Burke; Cummings and Eskes arrived at the same time. The expectant mother, said Eskes, was ready to deliver. He added that it might be a difficult birth. The three men wheeled the woman to the second operating room. Lita Cook was called from her apartment in case she were needed. Cummings bowed out gratefully before the greater obstetric experience of this team.

His respite was short-lived, however. A man limped into the waiting room with a bullet wound in his leg just above the knee. Two companions supported him on either side. They told Cummings that their friend had shot himself accidentally while drawing a pistol from his belt. All three were young civil militiamen from the checkpoints along the road to Port-au-Prince. Many times they had ordered Cummings and the other doctors out of cars, frisked them for weapons, and searched their baggage. The loutish routine had always irritated Cummings. He made no mention of this, however, as he gave the man a minute examination, and had him X-rayed, and his blood tested. The other two militiamen were also sampled for blood type; their friend had bled a great deal and might need a transfusion. The small blood bank at the hospital was running low.

When Cummings had removed the slug from the militiaman's leg, he studied the fellow's full laboratory report with a wry face. "Only in Haiti," he said, "would you admit a man with a bullet wound and find that he's much sicker with malaria and tuberculosis."

By this time St. Léger had finished in the delivery room. He was leaning against a wall in the passageway, smoking a cigarette. "Baby's dead," he said. "It was born with a heartbeat, but there was no cry. Phil and the anesthesiologist tried for an hour to keep the infant alive, but no good."

"There was nothing more you could do," Cummings said quietly.

"No," said St. Léger, rising to his full height, "but, by God, Paul, at times like this I feel inadequate. You know, when I started out in medicine I was full of idealism and confidence. That was in Gonaïves on the coast. I picked people off the streets and took them to my clinic. I tried to cure everyone—St. Léger, big man. But after three years I saw that I didn't know half enough to help the people who needed the help most desperately. So I went to study in the States, even got myself a master's diploma in Public Health, but now that I'm back again, I still find too many people I can't help. Every night I read medical books. Once I read Voltaire, Zola, all the great novelists, and listened to music. No more. Now I have time for nothing but medicine."

Gloomily he followed Cummings back to the ward to check on Sadius Seide. The peasant was muscular and seemed in good physical shape, but he was not responding to medical treatment. He still could not work his bowels and his stomach was hot and tense. His hands, however, were cold, so the doctors knew he was going into shock. For a long time they discussed the case and tried to calm the man's system. It was no use. Inside his abdomen something was very seriously amiss. Cummings decided, shock or no shock, he must open the abdomen for exploratory surgery.

Hospital rules required patients to authorize surgery. Sadius Seide, his face contorted with pain, "signed" the necessary document with a thumbprint. Then he was anesthetized and taken to the main operating room. All the power switches had been thrown, the lights, sterilizers, air conditioning. Andy Gallagher was standing by. The bleak, silent, gray-walled room was transformed into a modern surgery. When Cummings entered in blue-gray gown, cap, mask, and canvas boots, he might have been back at Massachusetts General in Boston.

Three operating-room nurses—Haitian, Filipino and American—were setting out the instruments and adjusting the patient so that his stomach was directly under the huge, low arc light. Lita Cook took her station behind the man's head and set up the breathing tubes. Cummings cut a deep incision in a shin for the blood transfusion. The patient's wrist was cut and taped to take the glucose solution.

Sadius Seide, an anonymous field worker from an unheard-of village named Gateneau, had been due for death this night. He was in shock, his blood pressure way down, his breath coming in tortured gasps. Cummings could see that his chance for survival was slender, but he must be given that chance. Months earlier, when Cummings was new to Deschapelles, a child had expired during his surgery. "Never mind," a veteran nurse had consoled him, "the kid's better off dead." Cummings had turned on the nurse angrily, his eyes smoldering above his mask. He did not say anything, but never again did nurses confuse Cummings' casual social manner with the ardor of the surgeon.

And now because he had a man's life at stake, he wanted to increase the odds against death. Going to the wall telephone, he called Hal May. It was eleven o'clock and May had gone to bed. Within six minutes, however, he was in the operating room ready to lead the surgery.

His scalpel flashed twelve inches down the tight, thin black skin of the man's stomach, laying open the white flesh and exposing the intestines. During four hours the two surgeons labored, one on each side of Sadius Seide. Only intense concentration kept them from becoming nauseated, for what seemed like yards of intestines had to be pulled out from the belly. The bowel, too, was twisted and blocked. It had to be cleaned and manipulated to a normal position.

All through this rummaging and untangling, the stench and squelch, and low mutter of May's voice, fresh life blood dripped silently into the arteries of the stricken peasant. At

3 A.M., when, mercifully, the stomach was being closed and sutured, the surgeons glanced anxiously at the empty bottle in the bracket above the man's leg. The blood had run out; there was no more in the bank. The patient desperately needed another pint to see him through the rest of the night.

His grouping was O-positive, the most common type—May's type. So after finishing the suturing, the chief surgeon went off to the blood donor room. That night he had given of his strength, his experience, his skill. Now he was going to give his blood.

Cummings took the patient back to the ward and instructed the nurses about the blood and glucose. The surgeons could do no more. Everything depended now on whether the spark of life left in Sadius Seide could be nourished into full flame again. Cummings was to wait nearly two days before learning that his patient could not come back.

But since he did not know this yet, and since his part in the life battle of Sadius Seide had been accomplished, Cummings' feeling of bone-weariness was almost pleasant. Walking across the lawn behind the wards, back to his apartment for three hours' sleep before another full stint of surgery, he smiled when he suddenly remembered a quip a surgeon friend had once made when asked what he had been doing all day: "Oh, same old routine—fighting disease and saving lives."

14

THERE IS a postscript to this brief narrative of Deschapelles. It concerns the contention of both Mellon and Schweitzer that a man does not need a medical degree and a swarm of diseased Haitians or Africans to practice humanitarianism and kindness.

Both men believe that as great or perhaps greater need exists for these same virtues among the loneliness and ugliness of harsh modern cities. They say: Give of yourself; extend a smile and a helping hand, and people will respond.

"What I am trying to do in Haiti," so Larry Mellon explained it to me, "you can do anywhere. The scale on which you do it does not matter. The important thing is to try."

I wondered about this, about how Mellon would express his ideals in a place like New York. Where would he start?

And then I received a letter from Gwen Mellon. She wrote:

> The subject is shoes, and inasmuch as you noticed Larry's and I forgot to tell you this story, here goes:
>
> Larry wears old shoes up to New York and buys a new pair there. He always looks the old ones over and says, "I don't think I'll carry these back. We have so much overweight." I'm always quick to agree as they really are usually pretty old and worn out.

Two years ago while we were in New York we went through this sequence one night as we were leaving to go out to dinner. On the way to the taxi, I saw that Larry was carrying a paper package. I asked him what it was and he said, "Never mind."

While we were driving along, Larry asked the taxi driver if life was tough these days. "Yes, very," said the cabbie. Did the driver have kids? "Yes, lots." Did he have boys or girls? "All boys."

"Well," says Larry, "here's something you might be able to use, a pair of shoes, not new, but still mileage in them."

The driver turned around and growled, "Now don't go leaving none of your stuff in my cab. I got no use for it." So we went to the dinner party with the brown paper package.

Well, just this year we were going out for dinner in New York on Eighty-first Street, all dressed up again, and Larry says he wants to stop on the way. I didn't ask why as he had a brown paper package under his arm. Off we went to a little Italian shoe-repairman near Bloomingdale's. I started to wait outside, but Larry wanted me to come in with him. The repairman stopped all his wheels and came over while Larry explained what he had. The man said, "Listen, buddy, no. I don't need any more shoes. I got two hundred pair inside."

This time we left the shoes in a trash barrel in the subway and went on up to Eighty-first Street. . . .

That is the end of the story. Or maybe it is the middle. I don't think Gwen Mellon has any doubts that her husband will try to give away the shoes he is wearing now.

Larry Mellon is not a man to be reduced by the surliness of the world—not in Haiti, New York, or anywhere else.